The Last Days of an Empire

By Len Mei

The Last Days of An Empire

To understand the way China behaves, it is essential to understand the national psychology of China.

To understand the national psychology of China, it is essential to understand the immediate past of China.

The Last Days of An Empire

The Last Days of An Empire

Dedication

This book is dedicated to my wife – Ana Maria.

Map of China in 1820

Contents

The Last Days of An Empire

Introduction

At the end of twentieth century, the world witnessed China's rise as a global power. Some alleged that the twenty-first century would be the Chinese Century. There are many reports and books to discuss the phenomena of China's rise. However, few realized that barely one hundred years ago, China suffered the lowest point in her history.

In the late nineteenth century, foreign powers dominated China. The only reason that China escaped the fate of being a colony is her sheer size. No foreign power would allow a single power to colonize China or to monopolize its interest in China. Meanwhile, no single power was large enough to colonize entire China. The talk on the table was how to divide China, when the revolution happened.

In 1823, U.S. President James Monroe declared the so-called Monroe Doctrine. It is a policy to prevent European powers to colonize further Latin America to damage the American interest. The United States reserved the right to interfere with such aggression. She issued a Doctrine at a time when many Latin American countries were on the verge of gaining independent from the Spanish Empire. The original intention of the Doctrine was for Latin America. By this Doctrine, the U.S. agreed that it would not interfere in European's existing colonies in exchange for the U.S. interest in America. The doctrine maintained that the New World and the Old World were to remain distinctly separate spheres of influence.

However, by the end of the nineteenth century, when the Eight-Nation Alliance (Russian, Britain, France, Germany, Italy, Austria, Japan and the U.S.) invaded China in 1900, after the Box Rebellion, the United States, as one of the eight powers invading China, interfered; feeling her interest in

Asia was threatened. The Eight-Nation Alliance could not agree how to divide their recent gains in China. Under the insistence of the United States per Monroe Doctrine, China could maintain her independence. It was called the "Open Door Policy." It literally meant that the door to China was open for anyone having an interest in China. Thus, the foreign powers were free to negotiate their interest in China without even consulting China. After Russia was defeated in the Russo-Japanese War, Russia transferred her rights in Manchuria to Japan. When German lost the World War I, she also transferred her interest in Shandong to Japan.

No country, even today, can withstand for long under the conditions imposed on China during the second half of the nineteenth century. Western Powers forced China to sign a series of unequal treaties to concede many rights. In addition to the loss of territories and outflow of billions of taels of silver as compensation to the lost war, China gave up the control of custom duty, opened the ports for free trade, forfeited the judiciary rights, and worst of all, was forced to allow the unrestricted importation of opium from British India.

The population in general naturally does not have resistance to the drugs, then or now. The unrestricted importation of opium for over one hundred years led to widespread drug addiction. The opium condemned China to the worst possible punishment. The evil of drugs created the problems down to the level of family, the very basic fabric of the society, generated poverty, decimated the productivity, lost the will to live, not to mention the outflow of the money for the opium consumed. British became the biggest drug lord the world had ever known. Opium trade

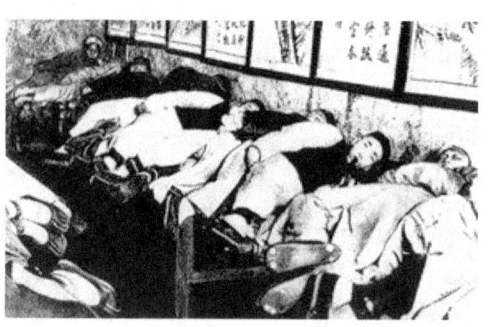

Figure 1 an opium house where people smoked

became the most profitable commodity trade, and was 20% of British revenue for over hundred years.

The war indemnity amounted to hundred millions taels of silver each time. The free trade essentially killed the nascent industry in China, dampened all the hope of a turn-around. While the industrial revolution was going on in full swing in the Western world, China was stagnant and impoverished beyond imagination.

The Christianity denounced the Chinese religions as superstition. The military invasion forced upon China the right to build churches and the freedom to preach Christianity. It was hard to convince Chinese that the Churches preached love. Foreigners and churches in China enjoyed special privileges and immunities from Chinese law. The resentment against foreigners was high.

However, China cannot blame everything on the foreign powers. China had multiple chances to reform herself just as Japan did. Even as early as the seventeenth century, during the reign of Emperor KangXi, Jesuit missionary were already traveling to China. The Jesuits brought with them the latest scientific knowledge from Europe, and were willing to share with the Chinese. However, at the height of Qing Dynasty, which considered itself as the center of the world, she had little interest in learning from the West. Some Jesuits were welcome to stay by impressing Qing Court with a display of ecclesiastical finery of the Western technology. Others endured imprisonment and deportation.

During the nineteenth century, while the Europe was advancing rapidly both economically and politically, China closed its door and refused to accept anything foreign for the next one hundred years.

The Opium War from 1839 to 1842 signaled a turning point in the Chinese history. When China realized the damages done by opium and sought to restrict illegal British opium trafficking in 1840, British declared war on China. China was ill prepared against the powerful British army. As a result, China lost the war. In addition, China was forced to open the door by the signing of the first unequal treaty in 1842.

The first encounter was detrimental because the Western Powers realized that China was an easy prey. She was much weaker than she appeared to be. Since then, China attracted more aggression and was going down the hill. China lost war after the war with ever more devastating effect. The imposed unequal treaties made the task of recovery even more difficult.

As an added misfortune for China, the synchronization of the dynastic cycles in the Chinese history further reinforced the downturn. The dynastic cycle is a unique, natural cycle in the Chinese history. In four thousand years of recorded Chinese history, a pattern dominated and persisted. The pattern is the dynasty cycle. History always repeats itself. In today's term, cycle is called "bubble."

In China, dynasties come and go. The force behind it was beyond the human control. A new dynasty always emerged out of chaos. The chaotic period could last from a few tens of years to hundreds of years, when China was fragmented. Constant civil wars, natural and man-made disasters, popular revolts, killed millions, until a strong leader emerged and unified China again.

If a dynasty did not suffer from infant mortality, it could last for hundreds of years. Strong and capable leaders always ruled a new dynasty. Moreover, the effort to rebuild the war-torn country inevitably increased the wealth. The mere fact that civil wars ceased after the unification helped to stabilize the society. Productivity increased. Food and merchandise became abundant. In addition, a reduced population, because of the prolonged civil wars, shared an increasing wealth. This also helped to enrich the individuals.

Hundred years into a new dynasty, both population and bureaucratic system swelled to a level that economic growth slowly became stagnant and the resources were scarce again. In addition, not all emperors were natural talented leaders. Power could fall into the hands of ambitious court officials, eunuchs or other royal family members, who abused the power for personal gains. Corruption became rampant and dynasty entered the downward cycle and suffered a long decline until the day that it could not sustain itself.

In the mid-nineteenth century, Qing Dynasty was already two hundred years old and was in the downside of its grand cycle. It was in natural decline, with or without the foreign invasion. However, the foreign invasion hastened its downfall.

Added to the complication, Han Chinese regarded Manchu people, the founder of Qing Dynasty, as a foreign power. The slogan of the revolutionaries at the time led by Dr. Sun Yat Sen was to "Expel the Tartar and Recover China." The Western invasion force could even get a helping hand from Han Chinese by purchasing the military food supply from them.

Manchu, who is an ethnic group belonging to Tungus branch of Altaic people distantly related to Turks and Mongols, invaded China in 1644 and founded Qing Dynasty.

After conquering China, Qing Court decreed to prohibit Han Chinese from entering the vast pastureland of their homeland, Manchuria. They reserved Manchuria for their eventual retreat, if one day, for some reason,

14

they had to leave China. Qing Court would severely punish any Han Chinese breaking the law. Until Manchu realized the ambitions of Japan and Russia, in the late nineteenth century, she opened the gate of Great Wall in the reverse direction to allow massive migration of Han Chinese into Manchuria. However, it was too late. Russia had already taken half of the Manchuria.

After the fall of Qing Dynasty, Manchu people lost their prestige. Many of them adapted Han Chinese names and mixed completely into Chinese. Today, even for those who claim Manchu ancestry, very few can speak Manchu tone.

It was easy for Han Chinese to blame Manchu for the demise of China. However, even if the Han ethnics were to have founded the last dynasty, China would have suffered the same fate, if not worse. Not only Manchu inherited the grand Chinese thinking as the center of the world and all the Confucius philosophy, but also Qing Dynasty produced better emperors than the average Chinese dynasties. The later Qing emperors might be incapable, but they were not corrupt. There were no shortages of the Manchu nobleman enthusiastically pushing for reform. Emperor GuangXu was the best example. Empress CiXi, who ruled China with iron hand for almost five decades, notoriously selfish and power hungry, was not on par with the last Ming emperors in corruption and ineptitude.

In addition, at the height of Qing Dynasty, during the reigns of KangXi, QianLong and YongZeng, over the period of hundred years, Qing expanded the Chinese history to be one of the largest among all the dynasties. It conquered Tibet, Mongol, and East of Siberia, a part of Central Asia and Taiwan and subdued Burma, Thailand, Laos, Vietnam and Korea into its vassal states. It was the empire with the largest continuous landmass in the seventeenth and eighteenth centuries. Despite the concession of huge territory in Siberia and Central Asia to Russia in the late nineteenth century, and the independence of Mongolia in 1946, China today is still one of the largest countries in the territory, thanks to the Manchu.

It is difficult to separate the China today from the China yesterday. China's fall in the nineteenth century was so unfathomable, that in spite of thirty years of miraculous economic growth since 1980, she is still a poor country in terms of per capita income. Only her sheer size makes her an economic giant. After reading this book, you might realize how difficult the task to restore China to her previous prosperity. From my point of view, it would need at least thirty more years.

The Last Days of An Empire

Is China today different from China yesterday? The political system may be different. One can argue that the essence remains the same. The Communist China is in the name of communism only. The Chinese communists cling to communism because it is their mandate of heaven, their justification to hold onto their power. It is the same mandate of heaven that dynasties justified their rules. Nothing that communist government does today is relevant to the communism that it preaches.

In order to contain the growing power of the new industrialists, Communist Party decided to recruit them into the Party. The Party can no longer represent the proletariats that it used to be. Many communists are rich beyond imagination. Furthermore, one can trace many of its policies back to the policies of late Qing Dynasty. For example, the state dominated private or public companies have their origin from the time of Li Hong Zhang, who invented this business model.

The culture always played a major role in shaping the way people think. People behave differently based on their culture background, education, and environment in general. The unique aspect of the environment of the upbringing of Chinese is the exposure to the Chinese history. This uniqueness is a quality of the continuity of her civilization. Chinese feel the ancient personalities two thousand years ago much more relevant than the Westerners feel about Roman nobles. Chinese today can read the books from two thousand years ago, which allow the Chinese today to identify with the past.

It does not matter whether the education is from opera or from TV. In the old times, the touring opera groups provided much of the history education to the mass in China. Even illiterate people could recite the stories of famous emperors in the past. Today, TV performs the same function. The TV programs are full of the episode of dramatized stories from all dynasties. The intrigues of the historical dramas fascinated people. Unconsciously, they behave accordingly. Even Mao, the founding father of the People's Republic, learned much of his tricks from the Chinese history books rather than from the "Manifesto of Communism."

Is the dynasty cycle broken with the arrival of modernization? Is the political party system free from the spell of the cycle of the imperial political system? Is Communist China one of the dynasties in China? It is too early to tell. After all, Qing Dynasty survived 275 years. If Communist China can survive that long as a dynasty, its end will not come until year 2245. If it indeed can survive as long as the last two dynasties, it will be a success. Otherwise, it would only be a short episode in the Chinese history, much like the Republic of China, which never really ruled China in her entirety in her brief history.

History is a sum of all the past events. However, history is more than the accumulation of random events. Every event has its own cause and effect. Cause and effect thread the events into a sequence. To understand the history, it is important to understand the sequence of cause and effect. I have written this book in the sequences of events by their causes and effects. It is much easier for the readers to understand why things happened the way it happened. In addition, it will make a more enjoyable reading. However, since many events are happening simultaneously, to follow the sequence of events by cause and effect is different as to follow the sequence of events by the time.

However, history is more than just cause and effect; random happenings knit them closely together. For example, if the little girl from a poor family, Laner, were not to have been selected as a concubine, she would not be one day become the absolute ruler of China for almost fifty years. If she were not to have been born with the talent, which allowed her to launch a coup at the age of twenty-six against the most powerful royal family members, defeated them and grabbed the power, when her husband died, China would also be different. Without being born with the extraordinary shrewdness, she could not have done it. Was her talent and wit an event generated by "cause and effect," I would say no. This kind of random coincidences is inexplicable, and adds another dimension to the history.

History also tells us: nothing is forever. A country or a civilization, like a living organism, will rise, grow, decay and die. China cannot avoid this cycle. However, China is unique in a sense that, besides India, it is only longest-lasting, continuous ancient civilization in the world. China achieves this feat by recycling, cleansing, and purging herself constantly so that after each down cycle, inevitably, she emerges stronger and richer. It is a built-in cycle. This was possible when China was an isolated civilization in the past. How, when China becomes a member of the much larger world, can this cycle continue?

History also taught us: whenever there is war, massacre inevitably followed. It is the human nature. China may blame the massacre of Nanjing by Japanese troop during World War II. However, less known to the world, barely ninety years before the Japanese Massacre, in a Chinese civil war, Taiping Rebellion, the same things happened. When the brutal killings in the

17

battlefield surround a man, it is difficult to keep a clear mind what is right and what is wrong.

The stories in this book are not for your history lessons. It is my intention to raise your interest to understand China by narrating the stories from a few important personalities during the epoch. These personalities are the household names in China, but outside of China, very few people have heard about them. They were very powerful people and held in their hands China's future. I want to shine lights on the key events during the downfall of Chinese empire. From the story, we can see that there was no lack of effort to reverse the tide, but it was an impossible task until something dramatic happened – the revolutions, not only once but twice.

I have written this book from many years of research into the subject of matter. I do not intend to write this book as a replacement of the history books. Rather, I want to condense the important events in the last sixty years of the Qing Dynasty into an interesting reading. I hope this book can provide those who are interested in China today to understand China of her immediate past.

The events in the book are mostly accurate to the historical records. It will serve as an introduction to you, and allow you further research into the subjects more interesting and easier.

However, there are events even the history does not provide a true account. In such cases, I used the most plausible scenario in my book. For example, Emperor GuangXu died at the age of thirty-seven just one day before Empress Dowager CiXi died. He fell into serious sickness suddenly on the day he died. Was this a coincidence? What is the probability of such a coincidence? Did he die of a nature cause or from murder? If he was murdered, who murdered him? Nobody knows. Maybe someday the truth will come out in this case.

On the day, that Empress Dowager CiXi exiled from Beijing to escape the Eight-Nation Alliance invasion, Emperor GuangXu's most beloved Consort Zeng fell into a well and died. Did Empress CiXi order the eunuchs to push her into the well? On the other hand, did Consort Zhen commit suicide? Again, nobody knows and nobody will ever find out. These are the riddles of the history.

In writing this book, the dates of events add a complication. Because the official calendar in Qing Dynasty is the Chinese lunar calendar, which is different from the Western calendar. In historical documents, the dates quoted for events could be using Chinese lunar calendar or Western calendar. The documents certainly do not explain which calendar they used. I could only compare the sequence of the events in each case to see which calendar makes sense. In some cases, if I could not discern the dates by the sequence of events, I skipped the dates.

The Chinese names used in this book follow the Pinyin system, which is a standardized and unified spelling in China today. In the older documents, you will find the names using other spellings. If you do research, you will have to reconcile the names. However, the well-known names remain unchanged. For example, Hong Kong is still called Hong Kong, not Xiang Gang, according to the Pinyin.

Lastly, I want to give credits to Wikipedia, Baidu and Google Earth for the pictures that I used in this book.

The Last Days of An Empire

The Last Days of
an Empire

The Last Days of An Empire

Chapter 1

Yuan Shi Kai

July first, 1905, seven years after the fateful and failed coup of Imperial Court by Emperor GuangXu, Yuan Shi Kai rode the train to Beijing. Yuan was the Viceroy of Zhili Province, where capital Beijing is located, and Minister of Beiyang (North Sea) in charge of the foreign affairs, external commercial, and defense for North Sea region. He was a rising star and one of the most powerful men in China.

Figure 2 Yuan Shi Kai

He was on his way to have an audience with Empress Dowager CiXi on the next day, and did not let anyone know his intention to visit the Imperial Court. He carried with him the proposal for reform. This proposal was a political reform to modernize China; however, it was also an instrument for his person gain in power. Yuan's personal ambition drove the proposal. It was a big political gamble for him. He would have to sell the proposal to the conservative Court, which was against any political reform. The proposal could lead him to be China's next ruler or to ruin his future or even cost his life.

Yuan had known well the fate of failed coup of reform launched by the innocent Emperor GuangXu seven years ago. Since such a reform would threaten the political power base of the conservative gang, headed by CiXi - the Empress Dowager, the adopted mother of the Emperor. GuangXu, even as an Emperor, ended up in confinement in the imperial palace for his role in supporting the reform. Other leaders of the reform were either executed or in exile. The Emperor himself had lost his personal freedom, not to mention his political power. The conservative gang was firmly in charge. Ironically, Yuan was the one who triggered the failure of the coup.

One day earlier, Yuan received an important piece of news in favor of his proposal. His political rival in the court, Wang Wen Shao, just resigned as the Staff of Grand Council, a position to help Emperor or Empress to manage the daily business of the court or affairs of the nation. Wang Wen Shao gave retirement as the reason. Qing Court promoted Yuan's good friend, Xu Shi Chang, to replace Wang. Qing Court also assigned Xu to act as the Head of Bureaucratic Administration. His promotions opened up a great opportunity to Yuan. To Yuan, the timing could not be better.

While Xu's promotion was not instrumental to his reform, nevertheless, he would gain an important alliance in the Court. Xu was a trusted friend. Yuan, while his ambition earned him many undesirable reputations, was always faithful to his friends. Xu was one of them.

Yuan Shi Kai was born in the village of Zhangying in Henan province in 1859. He came from a well-to-do family. He met Xu when he was eighteen years old, when he had failed twice to pass the provincial level of the Literature Exam, which hindered his desire of a political career.

The Literature Exam was a part of the Civil Service System had been the only way to pursue political career for ordinary people since Han Dynasty instituted it two thousand years ago. It was also an open channel for the government to select human resources nation-wide. With this system, any high-level position in the government, except the position of emperor, was attainable at least theoretically by any qualified Chinese. In fact, the history is full of the rag-to-rich stories of people from poor background to enter the highest office in the court by taking this career path. Therefore, millions of ambitious youths wanted to pursue such a dream and dedicated their life to study the materials required for the exam. The provincial Literature Exam was only the first step. After passing the provincial exam, one could attend higher-level Imperial Literature Exam in the Capital, where the candidates from all over China would compete.

Without other recourse after failing the exam, Yuan grouped together his colleagues of the same fate to organize a study group. Since he banked all the cost for the rent, books, instructors, his colleges elected him as the head of the study group. The study group met regularly to discuss poems, literature, political studies, and Western philosophies. Over the time, Yuan gained fame in his hometown.

At that time, Xu was a student in a nearby county, ZhunNing. He heard Yuan's fame and came to visit. When they met, they felt like old time acquaintances. They talked nonstop about literature, geography, politics, poems. Xu gladly joined Yuan's study group.

Since then, they became best friends. Xu always told other people, "I have met someone, who one day would do something great!" This "someone" was Yuan.

One day, Xu came to Yuan. He wanted to say something but hesitated. Yuan urged Xu, "What is that you want to tell me?"

Xu hammed and hawed, "I like to borrow some money from you. I will return it to you as soon as I can."

"Of course," Yuan injected, "May I know what is it for?"

Xu was afraid that Yuan would be unhappy if he told the truth, however, he took the courage, "I want to quit the study group and go to Beijing and continue my advance study there."

Yuan laughed: "This is small matter. I have the money you want. I will support you all the way."

Xu got this wish and was relieved. He went to Beijing and passed the Imperial Literature Exam. Soon he worked in the government. Eventually, Xu made his way to achieve the prominent position, owing to Yuan's support.

Now, Xu was a Staff of Grand Council and was in charge of the Administration, which was a newly formed ministry responsible for the new bureaucratic affairs.

Yuan exclaimed, "Finally the time of reform has come!" A political storm was gathering in Beijing. As much as the Imperial Court resisted the reform, the rising tide of events would force the change one-way or the other.

Fate of a Bystander

While Yuan traveled to Beijing, the brutal Russo-Japanese War, which lasted from 1904 to 1905, had barely ended. Two months ago, Japan had astonished the world and sunk the Russian Second Pacific Fleet in the Battle of Tsushima.

The Russo-Japanese War was detrimental to Russia but also a calamity for China as an innocent bystander. Qing Court declared neutral during the war. Nevertheless, the battlefields were on Chinese territory. China had suffered all the devastation of a war although as a bystander. The battlefields in Manchuria bore huge loss in human life and property damages.

The loathsomeness of the fiasco of the Jiawu Sino-Japanese War from 1894 to 1895 and the humiliation that followed by signing the unequal Maguan treaty, for which Qing paid dearly and conceded territorial rights including Taiwan and Liaodong Peninsula, were still deeply ingrained. Qing Court was hoping that Russia would teach Japan a lesson. However, the event turned out to be disappointing. Russian troop was suffering from one defeat after another. By March 10, 1905, Japan had occupied Shenyang, the largest city in Manchuria. Russian had causality over 90,000 soldiers. At the end of May 1905, as unthinkable as it was, in one battle, the Japanese Navy sank the entire Russian Baltic Fleet.

When the news unfolded, the world was taken by surprise. Qing Court was in shock. Barely ten years ago, Japan had defeated the newly and expensively equipped Beiyang Fleet. Now, it subdued army and nave of the mighty Russian empire. How was it possible?

Meanwhile, the defeat of Russia created chaos in Russia. People were revolting and demanding reform. The event ignited the fire of revolution. A wave of political and social unrest spread throughout the entire Russia. Qing Court saw the Russian Imperial Court as its own mirror image. Tsar Nicholas II was forced to set up a State Duma, the legislative assembly and adopt a certain form of a constitution.

The outcome of the Russo-Japanese War was a wakeup call for China. There were many discussions by political activists, who were advocating that it was not only a war in the battlefield; it was also a contest of the political system. A dictatorship could not compete with a constitutional monarchy, which Japan became one by the Meiji Restoration of 1866. Qing had lost the war to Japan ten years ago. Now Russia, which was viewed as one of the Western Powers, also lost the war to Japan. The disturbing events of uprising and strife in Russia could echo in China. Something needed to be done before it was too late. The revolutionaries led by Dr. Sun Yat Sen were already agitating overseas. Yuan saw this crisis as his opportunity to fulfill his lifetime ambition.

A Proposal

Yuan himself did not conceive the ideas of reform in the proposal. It came from his former professor in the Huai Army, Zhang Jian. Zhang was a renowned scholar and a prominent industrialist at that time. Years ago, he served General Wu Zhang Qing in the Huai Army as executive secretary, overlapping the time when Yuan also was in the Huai Army. Both went to Korea during the Korean uprising. Zhang himself was interested in the study of the political systems and had spent time in Japan to understand how the Japanese constitutional monarchy worked.

Figure 3 Empress CiXi

At the time, to advocate the idea of constitutional monarchy was dangerous. To the Qing Court, to implement such a political system meant to share the power with outsiders. The reformers proposed it during the Hundred Days' Reform, but had no chance to implement it. Zhang dreamed of such political reform. However, he was not in the position to push such reform. He thought Yuan could be a candidate to make it happen. Zhang did not have the faintest idea how Yuan would receive it. He sent a letter to Yuan.

To his surprise, Yuan responded his letter favorably. Yuan asked Zhang to give him the proposal. A few months later, after some back and forth discussion, Zhang incorporated some of Yuan's ideas, the proposal was finally ready to Yuan's satisfaction.

Yuan took the proposal with him to Empress CiXi on that fateful day. When he presented to the Empress CiXi, CiXi was surprised not at the proposal itself, but the fact that it came from Yuan. After all, Yuan was the one who betrayed Emperor GuangXu to kill the Hundred Days Reform in 1898, barely seven years ago. The memory of betrayal was still fresh in many minds.

At that time, Empress CiXi was taking vacation in the Imperial Summer Palace outside of Beijing. Many of the conservative gang was asking CiXi to stop GuangXu's reform. The Emperor entrusted Yuan using his Beiyang guards to blockade CiXi's communication with outside to buy more time for the reform. Unexpectedly, Yuan informed CiXi about GuangXu's plot in order to gain his personal privilege from CiXi. As a result, Empress CiXi cracked down, aborted the reform, and prosecuted the reformers. She also put Emperor GuangXu under house arrest. Yuan earned the reputation as traitor and became the most despised man in China.

Yuan presented the case very carefully and skillfully, while observing CiXi's reaction closely. He argued that the constitutional monarchy was the only way to save the throne. He cited Japan as example. After Japan's Meiji Restoration, Japan defeated even Russia, and of course, Japanese Emperor Meiji was still all-powerful. China could learn from overseas.

To Yuan's relief, CiXi agreed to study the proposal and issue an edict to solicit for more inputs. When Yuan's proposal became public, it was like a bombshell, exploded in the Forbidden City and nationwide. Zhang was both excited and worried.

Yuan's proposal immediately attracted media attention, both in China and overseas. It transformed Yuan instantly from a traitor to a reformer. The chief correspondent of Thames News in Beijing, Mr. Morrison, published the following reports, "Finally, China sees the light of reform," "Qing Empire has a powerful reformer -Yuan Shi Kai." Since then, Mr. Morrison followed Yuan everywhere, and became Yuan's political advisor later, when Yuan became the first President of the Republic of China.

Media in China also responded favorably. Many newspapers, which had criticized Yuan as traitor, now changed tones. Especially Zhang Jian wrote to Yuan with admiration.

However, there was only one person in the Court, who looked at Yuan with piercing eyes and suspicion. His glare made Yuan uncomfortable and worried. This person was Qu Hong Ji.

Qu Hong Ji

Qu was a Staff of Grand Council reporting to the Chief Staff of Grand Council, Prince Qingqing. Under Prince Qingqing, there were five Staffs of Grand Council – Qu Hong Ji, Xu Shi Chang, Rong Qing, Tie Liang, and Lu Zhuan Lin. All of them were in good terms with Yuan except Qu and the aged Lu, who was too old to care about anything. The Chief of Staff himself, Prince Qingqing, was particularly close with Yuan. He treated Yuan as one of his family members and discussed with Yuan any issue on hand. Qu felt isolated in the Grand Council.

Qu was watching Yuan as he performed. Qu dared not to speak out to expose Yuan's plot, but waited for a right opportunity. Qu knew Yuan was ambitious, and would sacrifice anyone for his own good. Qu's distaste of Yuan came two years ago.

One day a couple years before, Empress Dowager summoned Yuan to meet her in Yihe Garden Palace. Yuan came fully armed with his personal security guards. His awe-inspiring air was shocking. His guards holding weapons, dressing in bright yellow uniform decorated with tiger and dragon patterns were truly an awesome scene. It was more like a show of power rather than attending an audience with Empress. People in the Court were not accustomed to see such a rampant and arrogant display. Qu and Wang Wen Shao were watching the event afar, quietly observing the disturbance. They looked at each other, not knowing what to say. Qu and Yuan had not dealt with each other before, but from that moment on, Qu developed a deep antipathy for Yuan.

Qu's hometown was Zhangsha in Hunan Province. He came from a family with long history of public service. His father saw to himself that Qu became well educated to follow his path. In 1901, when CiXi came back to Beijing from a yearlong exile to flee the invasion of Eight-Nation Alliance, CiXi promoted him Qu into the Grand Council. That year, Qu was 52 years old. During his four-year service in the Grand Council, he had no accomplishment.

Qu was determined to make the defeat of Yuan's proposal as accomplishment. Qu knew that CiXi could not tolerate any person trying to gain his own influence and power using the name of reform. Qu knew well that Yuan's reform was nothing but a disguise for his ambition. Once uncovered, even with Yuan's influence, Qu was certain that CiXi's wrath would contribute the downfall of Yuan. Just like how she dealt with the Hundred Days' Reform several years ago. Even her adopted son, Emperor GuangXu, could not escape the punishment. Qu was so sure of it that the only thing he needed to do is to remain quietly and strike a deadly blow when the time came.

It turned out that the struggle between Qu and Yuan would damage both sides and seriously weaken the positions of Han people in the Qing Court.

Prince Qingqing

Meanwhile, the political tide had turned. In short span of seven years since the Hundred Days' Reform, both the world and domestic events forced CiXi to consider political reform, however reluctantly. Even Russia, one of the strong Western Powers, could not fight against the tide.

While CiXi might be more receptive to the reform, but she did not have was a workable plan. On the other hand, Yuan was not Kang You Wei and Liang Qi Chao, the leaders of Hundred Days' Reform, either. Yuan was a polished politician with well-connected network in the Imperial Courts, unlike the idealistic scholars Kang and Liang, who had known nobody in the court. From Yuan's point of view, the timing was perfect.

Over the years, Yuan's money also bought quite a few converts. Rumor said that Yuan's effort spared no high-level officials as his targets for contributions. Yuan used the occasions when they had major events at home, such as wedding, funeral, birthday party. Yuan used the money to buy favors that would not be possible without bribe.

Yuan's network also allowed him to collect vital information. He had implanted informers at every corner in Beijing, inside and outside of the Forbidden City. Rumors said that he even knew what CiXi was thinking.

Qu stayed in the Imperial Court, while Yuan stationed away from the Capital. Qu accompanied CiXi almost every day, while Yuan saw CiXi only once a while. Yet, Yuan knew more about what was going on in the Court than Qu did. This was the power of Yuan's network. This was the power of Yuan's information.

From 1905 to 1911, Yuan would experience several ups and downs in his career, and narrowly escaped critical situations miraculously unscathed. He was about to transform his political capital into the most powerful man in China. He would hold Qing Court as hostage to bargain with the Republic and mutated himself into a revolutionary like magic to become the first President of the Republic.

Since 1900, the overseas revolutionaries, such as Dr. Sun Yet-Sen, raised the banner to expel Manchu and restore China. It created an invisible gap between the Manchu and Han officers in the Court. They tried to avoid each other. However, only Yuan was the exception. Both Manchu and Han greeted him cordially when they saw him.

Prince Qingqing was in a good mood when he saw Yuan. His eyes brightened and so did his baldhead. His long beard trembled when he laughed. He must have received a sizable contribution from Yuan. He had news to tell Yuan.

Yuan's relationship with Prince Qingqing went back two years ago. Previously, Yong Lu, the then Chief of Staff of Grand Council, and Empress CiXi most trusted man, was Yuan's primary target for a contribution. Every time, when Yuan visited Yong Lu, Prince Qingqing complained that he only paid respect to Yong Lu and nobody else.

One day, the rumor from Imperial Court said that Yong Lu was seriously ill. Yuan visited him. Yuan then realized that Yong Lu often had taken sick leave for long and was not aware of many happenings in the Court. Yuan realized that Yong Lu would not fare very long.

After some small chats, Yong Lu unexpectedly asked him, "Did you see Prince Qingqing recently?"

The question surprised Yuan. He replied carefully, "No..."

Yong Lu looked at Yuan with a hint of sadness, and said, "I don't want to keep you for long. You should go to see Prince Qingqing."

Yuan realized that Yong Lu was giving him a lease of his political life. He was grateful to Yong Lu and departed.

Before he went to see Prince Qingqing, he prepared a bank note of considerable amount, and asked his first lieutenant Yang Shi Qi to deliver it to the Prince. When Prince Qingqing saw the note, he could not believe it. Prince was full of joy but declined, "How could I accept this?"

Yang had already prepared his speech, "Mr. Yuan told me that you would be the next Chief of Staff of Grand Council. To be in that position, you need to pacify the people around CiXi. This contribution is for you to smoothen your way to the court."

A few days later, Yuan visited Prince Qingqing at home. Prince Qingqing's son, Zai Zhen was also there. Yuan went up, holding Zai Zhen's hands and asked him about his study and his interests, like a big brother.

When Prince Qingqing saw it, an idea came to him and told Yuan, "Zai Zhen is still young. He needs much coaching. Why don't you consider him as brother to you?"

Yuan was elated, but he declined tactfully, "This is too much honor for me. Zai Zhen is a member of royal family. How can I be his brother?"

Prince Qingqing pretended to be insulted, said, "Don't be ridicules. There are marriages between Manchu and Han, why cannot you be brothers? If Zai Zhen has a brother like you, having prominent positions in the government, he is the one who is honored."

Yuan felt that it was the time to accept the offer, and smiled modestly, "If you insist, I would be more pleased to obligate."

Prince Qingqing laughed broadly, "Zai Zhen, toast to your new brother!" Among the toasts, the bond was sealed. Yuan gained a faithful and powerful political ally in Beijing.

Soon after, Yong Lu died, and as expected, Prince Qingqing assumed the position of Chief of Staff of Grand Council. Yuan never failed to patronize Prince Qingqing since then. In every occasion, such as Prince Qingqing and wife's birthdays, sons and daughters' weddings, grandson's first month celebration, Yuan arranged and paid for the ceremonies and parties, never left Prince Qingqing to worry about any expense.

Money talked, of course, Prince Qingqing also returned favors. Out of gratitude or out of necessity, he never failed to discuss important issues in the Grand Council with Yuan beforehand. Through Prince Qingqing, Yuan effectively exerted a great influence on the Grand Council.

CiXi

Earlier in 1905, Yuan received a piece of Court intelligence from his informants. It was quite unusual that even Yuan did not know what to take of it. The information revealed that Empress CiXi was considering a high-level political reform.

"How could that be? Is it reliable?" Yuan tended to dismiss it.

A few days later, another piece of intelligence came. It was more unsettling: "The Staff of Grand Council Qu Hong Ji recommended three times to pardon Kang You Wei and to recruit him for the reform." Kang was one of the leaders of the Hundred Days' Reform, a fugitive currently at large.

`What was unexpected was CiXi's response. She merely expressed displeasure and refused. To Yuan's understanding of CiXi, a provoking suggestion such as this should enrage CiXi. However, CiXi just expressed displeasure. Was there something changed in CiXi? The second news further confirmed the validity of the first one.

Yuan's mind was spinning fast. Was this a sign that CiXi finally accept reform? If the reform was to become the prevailing political trend in the Court, how Yuan could ride the wave and extract benefit from it?

However, before Yuan was to take any action, he had to confirm his suspicion to this reality. Yuan started to piece all the evidences together. At that time, Yuan was only forty-seven years old, but his agile reasoning allowed him to analyze the people's mind and motivation to a great depth.

Ten years ago, when CiXi had her sixtieth birthday, every provincial and Court officer was racking his brain to come up with gifts, which would give CiXi a long lasting and pleasing impression. Yuan was no exception. His tip came when he received a seemingly insignificant intelligence from the court. One day, CiXi was staring at wall in her quarter of the palace and contemplating. Finally, she left without saying anything.

When Yuan received this information, he took it seriously. An inspiration came to Yuan. He dispatched his servants to search for good paintings throughout the country. Finally, he selected one, framed it, and sent to CiXi as gift. Yuan spent the least amount of money and yet his gift was one of those more appreciated by CiXi. Every time when CiXi saw the painting on the wall, it reminded her of Yuan. This was what Yuan was capable.

Now, it was the time for the big test. In retrospection, Yuan could find traces of CiXi's acts that could piece together as an emerging intention for reform. It all started when CiXi was still in exile in Xian due to the Eight-Nation Alliance invasion of Beijing. She issued several edicts publicly to solicit proposals for reform. They attracted quite a few proposals, such as the proposals to establish Western style schools, to set up industries, to improve the economy, to found military schools, to build roads and railways, and many others. None of these was earthshaking. The reform indeed made some real progress here and there, but none changed anything fundamental.

To Yuan, CiXi never had any interest to do something good for the country. Everything she did was to preserve the power, her personal, her family and her dynasty power. Was this time any different? Yuan wanted to find out.

Lately, when he went to CiXi for audience, he noticed that CiXi was getting older. Time had etched in her facial expression, in her agility. She no longer was as sharp and acute as she once was. Her tone was softer and her manner was more appeasing. After all, she was seventy years old now. Suddenly, Yuan realized that her motivation for the constitutional monarchy reform was for real.

However, Yuan figured that CiXi had an entirely different motivation. Yuan theorized that with all that happened between her and the Emperor GuangXu, she could not let GuangXu regain power after she died. The only way was to set up a parliament with her own cronies to take away the power from GuangXu. Emperor GuangXu was only thirty-four years old. He certainly would outlive CiXi. As an Emperor, GuangXu definitely would regain power.

Thinking about GuangXu, Yuan could not help but tremble. Yuan knew that GuangXu would never forgive and forget Yuan's betrayal. One day, when Yuan had an audience with CiXi, GuangXu was present. Yuan tried to greet GuangXu, but GuangXu said sternly and coldly, "Yuan, I know that you are thinking." Yuan avoided GuangXu's stare of despise and hatred. Yuan then knew that the last day of CiXi would be his last day also.

Later, Princess Der Ling, who served as CiXi's personal assistant and translator, would write in her memoirs entitled "Two years in the Forbidden City" about Yuan as perceived by GuangXu: "I stared at him. The traitor would not look up; he knew what kind of damage he had caused. He was pale and looked at the ground. His expression clearly showed that he was frightened either by me or by his conscience."

Four years ago, when CiXi and GuangXu returned from Xian to Beijing, CiXi asked Yuan to clean up palace for Court's arrival, while staying in a temporary residence for a few days. Again, Yuan asked his first lieutenant

Yang Shi Qi to watch closely how GuangXu held up himself as he returned to Beijing. What Yang reported to Yuan concerned him.

When the Court officers discussed the repair of Heavenly Gate to the Forbidden City, which was destroyed by the Eight-Nation Alliance invasion, GuangXu said, "To me, we do not need to repair the Gate. It will serve as a remembrance to us."

When CiXi restored the theater in the Forbidden City after their coming back from exile and asked to show the first opera, GuangXu commented: "How could we enjoy the show at this time when our country has not recovered from the invasion yet?"

In a different occasion, when a eunuch went to collect dirty laundry from Emperor, the eunuch found a dirty, worn vest. As the eunuch wanted to pick up the vest, GuangXu stopped him, "Don't. I wore this vest all way from Xian to Beijing. It had not been cleaned for month. I want to keep it this way as a souvenir."

These tiny episodes clearly showed how GuangXu could not forget any of the mishap. How deeply they were etched into GuangXu's mind and heart. What happened next served as reminder that Yuan was not the only one who felt this way.

In the temporary residence, CiXi's room was well furnished with purple-red sandalwood bed with stately headboard, covered with silk quilt warm and cozy. Even the room of Li Lian Ying, CiXi's head eunuch, was comfortably furnished. Li Lian Ying was GuangXu's most despised person, who played CiXi's ear by gossiping everything about GuangXu.

Li Lian Ying had certainly played an important role in the murder of GuangXu's most loved concubine Consort Zhen, when the Court fled the invasion of Eight-Nation Alliance in 1900. The sight that Consort Zhen was pushed into a well and then covered by stone plate and let die, while GuangXu watched helplessly was unbearable to him even many years later. Everything was taken away from him, his power, his freedom, even his beloved wife. Since then, GuangXu had become withdrawn, and fully immersed in himself, lived the life of a living dead.

GuangXu's quarter was barely furnished; bed with hardwood board, thin and dirty quilts, a wooden chair, nothing much. Li Lian Ying did something surprising. At night after CiXi retired into her quarter, he showed up in GuangXu's room, and greeted GuangXu. Li asked GuangXu why he was up so late at night. GuangXu laughed sarcastically; "How could I sleep this way."

Li looked around and found that GuangXu did not even have the barely necessity to keep warm in this cold weather. Li immediately blamed himself, "Dame me that I did not take care of your Majesty." He left and soon came back with warm quilt to GuangXu.

It seemed that Li was truly whole-hearted to serve GuangXu. Yuan suspected that Li was mending his fence with GuangXu in preparation for the eventual future when CiXi would die. The future was not too far away.

Yuan made a test to confirm his suspicion. On Yuan's birthday, Yuan invited hundreds of guests for his birthday party. Their names were like the list of who is who in Beijing. At the end of the party, when all the guests were gone, Yuan invited Li to stay. Now the night was deep and everything was quiet, Yuan arranged delicacies and aged liqueur to entertain Li. Li was not stupid. He knew Yuan wanted to ask him a favor. He said," I am only a servant. Why your Honor treat me so highly?"

Yuan said, "It is nothing. I want to take this chance to give my greetings to Empress CiXi. I heard that she does not feel well lately. You stay with her every day. Surely you take good care of her."

Li said, "Empress knows your kindness. She also sends regards to you."

Suddenly, Yuan bowed deeply to Li, said sincerely, "You are most loyal to Empress. When I see you, it is like I see Empress herself."

Li was abashed, and supported Yuan with hands and raised him. "Please don't embarrass me. You are the one Empress CiXi likes the most. Otherwise, how could you be promoted so fast?"

Yuan said modestly, "This, of course, it was all your effort."

Li was flattered. He followed by describing Empress CiXi's wellness.

While listening, Yuan dropped tears, "We all pray that Empress can be well forever. Otherwise, there will be no us."

Li sighed, and said, "I realized it long ago." He did not want to say anymore and said goodbye.

The next day, CiXi received Yuan's audience, and comforted Yuan:" You don't have to worry about your job." Yuan felt like to cry.

This happened one year ago. After confirmation from many aspects, Yuan had no more doubt about his theory. Yuan was looking for a way out. Yuan spent one year to study and investigate the parliamentary system. The more he studied, the more he was convinced that it was an excellent plan. In the parliamentary system, there was a cabinet. The head of the cabinet was the prime minister. The prime minister held the effective executive power. There was also the congress and the judiciary branches of the government. The emperor effectively was a figurehead with no real power. Yuan already assumed that he would be the prime minister and Yuan would fill the congress and judiciary branches with his cronies. He even already had the candidates in mind for these positions. The parliamentary system was the magic bullet. He was amazed at the genius who invented the parliamentary system. Zhang Jian proposal came at the right time.

It now became quite clear to Yuan that political reform was his only chance of his survival. It had to be done quickly. The time was pressing.

Yuan did not want to second-guess CiXi anymore. He had realized by now that CiXi was not against reform. She was against sharing power with others. He not only wanted to confirm with CiXi but also to lead CiXi down the path of reform. Yuan was convinced that if the reform were to carry according to CiXi's way, CiXi would agree. Yuan realized that if the parliament was not established and his cronies were not in control of the congress and judiciary system when CiXi died, his days would be numbered.

Yuan considered carefully the timing of this political reform. He set the period to be twelve years to accomplish his goal -that is, to implement the Constitutional Monarchy system, like the one in Japan. If it was done too soon, CiXi might not want to relinquish her power. If it was done too late, CiXi might die before the system would become mature enough to prevent the comeback of GuangXu.

Yuan believed that CiXi would be unlikely to live for twelve more years, as she was already seventy years old. When all done, Yuan would be the prime minister firmly in control of the congress and the judiciary branch. In another word, he would be the supreme ruler of China at fifty-seven years of age. GuangXu would be nothing but a figurehead. His desire burned feverishly. He wanted to be in control of the events rather than drifting with the events. He wanted to coerce CiXi to do so. He wanted to set the motion to change the course of the history.

Now the proposal was out. Persuaded by Yuan, Zhang Zhi Dong and Zhou Fu, two of the heavy weight officers, also endorsed the proposal.

Zhang was the Viceroy of six Provinces in Southern China. He built his reputation to the founding the heavy industry in modern China. On the other hand, Zhou was the Viceroy of Nanyang (South Sea), counterpart of Yuan in command of the Beiyang. Zhou was also considered as the founding father of the Chinese military school. Yuan included them both for increasing his impetus and as a buffer.

On July 5, 1905, Empress CiXi approved his grand proposal. As expected, the media all over China gave Yuan's reform proposal a warm welcome. Even his critiques were silenced.

Fourteen days later, on July 16, CiXi selected Baron Zhen Ze, Secretary of Interior Dai Hong Ci, Staff of Grand Council Xu Shi Chang, Viceroy of Hunan Duan Fang, and on July 27, added Deputy Minister of the Commerce Department Shao Ying, to be the high-level government delegates to travel overseas to investigate the Western parliamentary political system. Everything was moving at a fast pace. It looked like the political reform was finally for real this time.

Terrorist Attack

September 24, 1905, a day of celebration turned into a day of mourning due to a terrorist attack.

Everything started beautifully on that day. It was a fine autumn day - bright sun with a smooth breeze. The weather was pleasant - neither too hot nor too cold. Five delegates for the mission of reform investigation would depart from Beijing train station to take the long trip overseas. This was a major event in China. Never so many high- level officers had traveled overseas for such an important mission.

A large farewell crowd gathered at the station, saying goodbye to the delegates. The delegates were dressing in Qing Court official costumes – with embroidered silk decorative patterns, the horse-hoof shaped sleeve, and the Mandarin jacket. Amid the animated band music and crowd noise, suddenly, the sound of explosion rocked the station. Smoke and debris were everywhere. Station immediately plunged into chaos. Crowd was shouting and crying. People were rushing around and running aimlessly. Polices and security guards hurried to the scene and found several bloody and mutilated bodies nearby the wrecked train. One of the bodies carried an ID identifying him as Wu Yue. Other bodies appeared to be innocent bystanders.

Among five delegates, only two -Zai Ze and Shao Ying were hurt. Others were shocked but otherwise unscathed. However, the trip had to be cancelled. Several days later, the police identified the dead terrorist Wu Yue as a revolutionist, acting as a lone suicide bomber. He was affiliated with Dr. Sun Yat Sen -the famous head of the revolutionary party.

Even though the event casted a shadow on the reform, but the determination was not damped. Nevertheless, two of the delegates had to be replaced – Xu Shi Chang and Shao Ying. Xu was appointed to lead the newly organized national police force, and Shao Ying, hurt in the explosion, refused to take the trip. Shang Qi Heng, the Chief Political Commissioner from Shandong, and Li Sheng Duo, Mayor of Suentian, replaced them. Finally, they were set to go.

Rumors said that the bomb was only a warning. When the delegates were overseas, revolutionaries plotted to assassinate them all. In order to pacify the delegates, CiXi hosted a farewell banquet. She encouraged the delegates, "Our country's hope is pinning on you now."

The delegates replied -their duty was to serve the Empress and the country. They would be willing to face any danger without turning back. CiXi was highly delighted.

The revolutionaries did not expect that the bombing event greatly raised the reputation of Qing Court. Western media was reporting favorably the reform and the reformers -especially Yuan. They labeled Yuan as the greatest reformer of China. They even compared him to the Japanese Ito Hirobumi, who was the key architect of the Meiji Restoration thirty-seven years ago. News also said that a bomb was found in Yuan's carriage. Fortunately, his security guard discovered it early enough so that the bomb did not kill anyone. Whether this was true or fabricated, nobody would know. However, it indeed raised Yuan's reputation to a higher level.

Police

Thanks to the bombing incident, Qing Court decided to form the nation-wide police organization. On October 8, 1905, Chinese police force was officially born. The Qing Court assigned the Staff of Grand Council Xu Shi Chang to lead the effort of creating and establishing a nation-wide police organization. The system borrowed the model of Tianjin police department, which was a local organization set up by Yuan. Yuan was

19

credited as the father of Chinese police system. Tianjin's chief of police - Zhao Bin Jun, a Yuan's crony -of course, had the most experience in organizing the police affair. He was appointed as the executive chief of police in the newly created police department.

The police system in Tianjin had a humble and humiliating start. It had been four years ago. In 1901, Qing Court signed an unequal treaty with the Eight-Nation Alliance after the defeat, paying huge compensation and conceding many trading rights and territory lease. After the treaty, Qing Court appointed Yuan as the Mayor of Tianjin, the port where the invasion started and the city with international settlements. Yuan had a dilemma. The unequal treaty did not allow China to station an armed force within twenty miles from the city center. Without maintaining the armed force, it was impossible for the city government to maintain law and order. Furthermore, Tianjin was the entry point of Beijing, the Capital. Without any defense in Tianjin, the door to the Capital was wide open. It exposed Beijing to another invasion without even a buffer. However, Yuan could not do anything to change the treaty.

It gave Yuan opportunity to demonstrate his ingenuity. He selected three thousand soldiers from his army and outfitted them with police uniform, and officially called them the Police. At that time, Chinese did not know what police was. Yuan led these three thousand soldiers in the police uniform to enter the city. The Eight-Nation Alliance was speechless. The idea of the police system came from the West. There was no violation of the treaty. Westerners were at lost to complain.

Within two years, the city's crime rate dropped significantly. Even foreigners were at awe of the performance of the police. Thus, the Chinese police system was born.

Initially, Yuan did not have any experience with the police system. He had thought that police was no difference from the traditional Chinese security guard. Later, Yuan learned that police could perform many other functions, such as the check of the household registration, protection from fire, arrest of petty thieves, supervision of food hygiene, arbitration of civilian dispute, issue of tickets for the minor violations, street patrol, detective work and others. It took many burdens off the civic duty from the city administrator. Yuan's police system even comprised some of the later day's judiciary duty.

1902, Yuan assigned Zhao Bin Jun as the principal of Bao Ding Police Academy, and recruited Miura -chief of police of the Tokyo Police

Department as a consultant and principal instructor. Yuan realized that the modern police system was much more functional than the old time Chinese security guard system. However, it required rigorous training and management.

In 1904, Yuan elevated the Bao Ding Police Academy to be Beiyang Advanced Police College, and reported the result to the Qing Court. Qing Court soon appointed the Beiyang Advanced Police College as the nationwide model of police school.

Yuan also included prison into the police system as early as 1903. On April 29, 1903, he proposed to Qing Court to set up the prisoner training school. It was modeled after the Japanese prisoner training system. The curriculum of the prison system was soon included in the Police Academy.

Setting up the police system also brought forth the reform of judiciary reform. Utilizing the national police administration set up after the terrorist bombing in 1905, Yuan created law schools designated for the judiciary training of the newly appointed officers. Some of the selected students were sent to study in Japan and assigned government positions when they returned. In 1907, Yuan established the first Chinese judiciary court in Tianjin.

Xiang Army

October 21, 1905, less than two weeks after Qing Court set up the National Police Administration, Yuan held military parade of his Beiyang armed force. Yuan's army was the pillar of Qing's power. He built it; he owned it and it listened only to him. Throughout his career, Yuan had changed many posts and titles, but his army was never detached from him. Foreign presses credited him as the "Greatest Chinese Military Expert." Later, Yuan would escape of execution because his private army was behind him.

Yuan started his military career early. Twenty-four years ago, May 1881, when Yuan was barely twenty-two years old, he was wondering around deciding what to do. He could not decide whether he should pursue his study or do something else, until he read a book -"The Chronicle of Xiang Army (Army of Hunan Province)," which changed his life.

"The Chronicle of Xiang Army" was a biography of Zeng Guo Fan, the founder of Xiang Army. When Taiping Rebellion was rampant in 1852,

Qing Court encouraged the regions occupied by Taiping Rebellion to organize their own armies to defend themselves.

Zeng, as the Senior Deputy Secretary of the Board of Rites, was already a mid-level administrative officer in Beijing. He saw it as his career opportunity, even though he never had any military experience. In 1852, financed by Qing Court, he organized a military training school in his hometown. It was the beginning of Xiang Army. Quickly, he expanded the Xiang Army by throwing himself into battlefields.

After several earlier defeats, Zeng was able to lead successful campaigns to recapture the capital city of Hunan, Changsha, from Taping Rebels. Within one year, he recovered Wuchang, Hanyang and Hankou, a tri-city of major trading ports in the mid-stream of Yangtze River. Qing Court acknowledged his victories by decorating him with yellow riding jacket, a high honor for military personnel, and he gained fame nationwide. He was renowned for his ruthless punishment of his subordinates and was merciless to his enemies. He gained a nickname "Zeng, the head cutter" for his senseless slaughter.

When he recaptured Nanjing from Taiping Rebels in 1864, he slaughtered young and old in ten thousands, mostly civilians. He looted the Taiping court for all the valuables and yet reported to the Qing Court that he found nothing valuable. He also burned down the city for three days and three nights. His cruelty was beyond description. A popular saying went that the most effective way for the mothers to stop baby crying was to say, "If you don't stop crying, Zeng, the head cutter, will come." His Xiang Army successfully vanquished the rebellion and saved the Qing Court. He became the hero of Qing Court.

Zeng's story of Xiang Army inspired Yuan. Zeng was able to achieve his fame within a short span of two years from an obscured mid-level government official to a commander of the most powerful army in China. Yuen decided to join the army. He wanted to follow Zeng's footsteps.

At that time, Xiang Army no longer existed. However, Huai Army, Army of Anhuei Province, was a powerful fighting force. Zeng's disciple, Li Hong Zhang, founded it.

Li Hong Zhang was a controversial person in Chinese history. He received both praise and criticism. He was Yuan's predecessor of the Viceroy of Zhili and Minister of Beiyang. He was the principal negotiator of many unequal treaties with foreign powers. The population in general criticized him for being too soft and giving up to much in the negotiation. The country did not appreciate what he had done. However, he was also credited for laying the foundation of modern Chinese industry, and building the modern Chinese navy.

Yuan's father had an old friend, Wu Zhang Qing, from the same hometown. Wu was a general in the Huai Army. When Yuan decided that he wanted to follow Zeng's career, he went to see Wu.

Wu was happy to keep Yuan with him. He had known Yuan since a child. For a while, Wu did not have much for Yuan to do. Nevertheless, Yuan was doing his homework by paying attention to every detail of the operation of Huai Army. Before long, the opportunity came. It was August 7, 1882. An edict arrived in DengZhou where Wu stationed his Huai Army. It ordered Huai Army to move to Korea immediately to put down the rebellion in Korea by the request of King of Korea.

A political struggle between King's father Daewongun and King's wife Queen Min triggered the event. In July 1882, there was a food shortage in the garrison, and the angry soldiers and mobs soon turned a demonstration into a riot. Soldiers looted the warehouses and granary, which belonged to Queen Min, and opened them to the mob. When Daewongun took the advantage to dispatch his army in the name of maintaining order to enter Queen Min's palace, the turmoil spread into a full-scale fight. Queen Min fled by disguising as a palace servant. While in hiding, Queen Min asked Qing Court for rescue and help. Two weeks later, Huai Army received the edict.

Ever since the Meiji Restoration, Japan had been eyeing to take control of Korea. Japan had been long waiting for an excuse and the right opportunity. During the riot, the mob attacked the Japanese embassy, and the ambassador fled back to Japan. It was a perfect excuse. Quickly, Japan decided to dispatch its military force to Korea. By August 10, three days after Huai Army received the edict, Japan's fleet was approaching Incheon port. Huai Army had only a few days to mobilize.

Huai Army had made the meritorious contribution during the pacification of Taiping Rebellion. It had established its name for bravery and tactfulness. Taiping Rebels were out of control across a country for fourteen years, and estimated sixty million people perished. Without Xiang and Huai Armies, Qing Dynasty would not have survived. It instilled the arrogance in both Armies. However, Taiping Rebellion had been forty years ago. Zeng Guo Fan dissolved his Xiang Army after the put down of Taiping Rebellion.

Huai Army also lost its spirit as a fighting machine after a long period of peace. When Qing Court called its founder Li Hong Zhang into the court for other services, he entrusted his subordinates to take care of the Army. None of them was as capable as Li, and it gradually corroded into a paper tiger.

When Yuan joined the Huai Army, the Army was in disarray. There was no discipline. The lack of training and obsolete weaponry rendered Huai Army incapable. The fighting spirit of the glorious old days was gone. Yuan had a natural talent in the military affairs. He had perceived much of the shortcoming. When Wu received the edict to mobilize his troop to Korea in seven days, he realized that it was nearly an impossible task.

Yuan seized the opportunity and went to see Wu. Yuan said, "General Wu, how are you going to mobilize your troop to travel across the sea and fight in a foreign country in such a short notice? You don't even have the logistics ready for the supply for food and weaponry."

Wu was surprised at Yuan's initiative and thoughtfulness. Yuan had pointed out exactly what Wu was worried. He asked," What do you suggest?"

Since Yuan had been observing the operation, training and logistic aspects of the Huai Army, he was well prepared to answer Wu's question. He then pointed out to Wu what he saw as the shortcomings of the troop, what would be needed to take the expedition, how could one prepare the war overseas. Wu was overwhelmed, and admired this young man for his wisdom and initiative. He immediately assigned Yuan for the task of preparation for the expedition. This embarked on Yuan's first military success.

Yuan exercised his newly acquired power to apply discipline. At that time, gambling was rampant in the garrison stations. Soldiers left the camp at night to fool around in the city and came back late and drunk, if they came back. They would disobey the call for drilling. Yuan caught a few violations and acted on behave of General Wu to punish offenders severely, and then reported to Wu later. It soon achieved the desired effect.

Yuan also worked feverishly to plan the detail of logistics. Miraculously, the troop departed on August 20 1882, only two weeks after receiving the edict. It arrived in Korea one day later.

When Huai Army arrived in Korea, Japan already anchored several war ships outside of the Incheon harbor. The arrival of Qing' s army took

Japanese by surprise, and apparently, Qing overpowered Japanese troop. General Wu took a quick decision to land in Korea immediately.

Using both superiority in manpower and political coercer, Huai Army successfully rescued Queen Min and restored her power. Wu arrested Daewongun, Queen Min's rival and the leader of the pro-Japanese faction, and in order to prevent the same thing from happening again, Wu escorted Daewongun to China and house-arrested him in Bao Ding.

At the same time, in order to avoid a direct conflict with Japan, Wu also allowed Queen Min to sign a compensation agreement with Japan. The peace in Korea was temporarily restored.

For the success of Huai Army expedition, Yuan's reputation was quickly widespread and his military talent was recognized. He received a consequential promotion.

Yuan realized that Huai Army could not stay in Korea for long. The long-term solution was to enforce and consolidate the power base of pro-China faction in Korea. Among many other implementations, Yuan agreed to train Korean troop.

However, the thirst of Japanese ambition could not be quenched.

Twelve years later, in the year of Jiawu, 1894, another revolt happened in Korea. Korea requested Qing Court to help again. However, this time, Japan was well prepared. A full-scale war exploded between China and Japan. It was the famous Jiawu Sino-Japanese War. China suffered a total defeat. It rocked the foundation of Qing Court.

The Last Days of An Empire

Chapter 2

Li Hong Zhang

Li Hong Zhang, the founder of Huai Army, was born in 1823. His father was the contemporary and a friend of Zeng Guo Fan, the founder of Xiang Army. In 1895 during the fateful Jiawu Sino-Japanese War, Li, as the Viceroy of Zhili and the Minister of Commerce of Beiyang, was the supreme commander of the Chinese army and navy. He was the most trusted Han officer of Empress CiXi.

When he was twenty years old, he was selected as the outstanding student in his home district and was sent to Beijing for advanced study. At the age of twenty-four, he passed the Imperial Literature Exam, and became as the member of Imperial Academy, where he was a disciple of Zeng Guo Fan. He had made many acquaintances in the academic and political circles in Beijing through his father's and Zeng's networks. His career and his political affiliation were heavily influenced by his acquaintances, especially Zeng. Zeng always praised him as the young man with multiple talents and capabilities.

When Taiping Rebellion started in 1851, Li was only twenty-eight years old. Qing Court encouraged people in the province to organize local army to defend their own land from Taiping Rebels. Zeng, at that time, as a middle level officer in Qing Court, saw the opportunity and took Li with him. They went to Zeng's home province, Hunan also known as Xiang, and started to organize a self-defense troop. Later, it became the famous Xiang Army.

Within two years of the founding of Taiping Heavenly Kingdom, Taiping Rebels swept from its founding place in Guangdong, southern China to Yangtze River region. Wherever the Taiping Rebels army passed, the corrupted Qing army could not resist. In 1853, Taiping Rebels took Nanjing and established its capital there. Almost half of China fell into the hands of Taiping Rebels. If the trend continued, Taiping Rebels could reach Beijing, Qing's Capital, within two years. Qing Court became very shaky.

Li started his military career by serving Zeng in the Xiang Army. Later, in 1860, on Zeng's order, Li took the responsibility to branch out Huai Army. Huai, or Anhui, was his hometown. Soon, Huai Army became Li's private army. By 1862, Li's Huai Army was 70,000 men strong, and Li recruited foreigner mercenaries in Shanghai and deployed modern weaponries. In effect, Li's Huai Army became China's first modern army, in organization, training, as well as weaponry. Huai Army survived Qing Dynasty, and evolved into armies of warlords after the founding of Republic.

When Li arrived in Shanghai for the first time, Shanghai was already a city of riches. It was a cosmopolitan city, a major trading port between China and the West. The business was thriving and the Western influence was strong. That set apart Shanghai from other Chinese cities, both in appearance and in substance. It was also the outpost of Western Powers in China. There were many foreign concessions where the Westerns congregated. In early 1860's, Taiping Rebels was planning a large scale of attack on Shanghai. Foreigners in Shanghai were clearly worried.

At that time, Shanghai had its own defense force "Shanghai Defense Bureau," which was led by an American Frederick Townsend Ward. It employed foreign mercenaries with advanced weaponry and

Figure 4 Li Hong Zhang

excellent training. When Li's Huai Army first arrived, his soldiers wore ragged and worn-out uniforms. Shanghainess ridiculed them as "bagger's army." Soldiers in Huai Army were quite upset.

Li told them, "Let us show them our strength."

They did not have to wait for long. Within months, Taiping Rebels invaded Shanghai. Huai Army under the leadership of Li defended the west outskirt of Shanghai -Hongqiao, Beixinjing and Sijiangkou. After brutal battles, Huai Army successfully drove out the enemy. Huai Army thus gained respect from the Shanghai community -both Chinese and Westerners.

Li' s stationing in Shanghai exposed him to the superiority of Western weaponry and training for the first time. He realized that it was the only way to go to improve Huai Army. He reformed his army by recruiting Western military experts and mercenaries as coaches for training and purchased modern weaponry from the West. Soon, Huai Army transformed from the backward traditional Chinese army into a well-equipped and trained modern army. By doing so, Li had greatly raised the combating power of Huai Army. He also reorganized his staff, replacing the staffs and commanders who could not bring themselves up to date, with those who were apt to accept the new concepts -Westernized military tactic and technology. Since then, Huai Army evolved into a different kind of army from Xiang Army. It signaled a beginning of the modernization of Chinese military.

In order to defend their foreign concessions, British general William Staveley teamed up with Frederick Townsend Ward to fight against Taiping Rebels near Shanghai. This army was nicknamed as Ever Victorious Army, because it was quite successful in the combat. It consisted of Western commanders and recruited Chinese soldiers. When Ward was killed in a combat, William Staveley recruited Charles George Gordon to take over the commander position.

Gordon was a very controversial person. He was the commander of British-French Alliance Invasion to China in 1860 during the second Opium War. He was the one who ordered the senseless burning of Yuanming Palace, which was considered as the crime of the century by the Chinese. China and the world at large had lost a valuable treasure. In May 1862, he was transferred to Shanghai, and soon, he took over the commander position in the Ever Victorious Army.

Taiping Rebellion

The Taiping Rebels were a strange mix of Chinese traditional canon and Christianity. It caused a widespread civil war in China from 1850 to 1864. On one hand, it represented the Han Chinese to rebel against Manchu rule, therefore, received many supports from ordinary people. On the other hand, traditional Chinese, like Zeng Guo Fan, rejected its adoption of the Christian religion as the banner. Although the leader Hong Xiuquan was a converted Christian, he was not affiliated with any Western churches. In fact, the teachings of the Taiping Rebels were entirely homebrew, borrowing the concepts from the Bible and yet mutated into a strange sect, not unlike many Chinese cult with the mix of Buddhism, Taoism and Confucianism. Hong Xiuquan claimed that he was Jesus Christ's younger brother, a fact not acceptable to the Westerners. Therefore, not only he did not get any support and sympathy from the West, but also in the end, the Westerners helped Qing Court to crush the Taiping Rebellion.

Hong himself, also a by-product of the Literature Exam System, failed to pass the Exam several times, and therefore, was resentful of the existing system. Once his serious illness was cured after reading a material from Church, he claimed that his heavenly brother Jesus Chris had saved him. Moreover, Jesus sent him to overthrow the Manchu dynasty and to save China. Before long, he adopted the teaching of the Bible with many traditional Chinese religious rituals, so that population at large could accept it easily. In one sense, he was more successful to preach the Christianity than the churches because he repackaged the Christianity with Chinese coatings. Soon, he attracted thousands of followers.

In early 1851, he organized a ten-thousand strong rebel army to stage an uprising. The uprising itself was nothing new to the Qing Court. Every few years, somewhere in the empire, there were one or more uprisings. However, the Taiping uprising was different. It soon escalated into a full-scale civil war, at the time, American Civil War was also raging on across Pacific.

Taiping Rebels' force continued to grow until it took Nanjing in 1860 and proclaimed the founding of Taiping Heavenly Kingdom with its capital in Nanjing. However, since then, the internal power struggle prevented from being effective in the campaign. Its failure to take Shanghai signified the turning point against the Taiping Rebels.

Li's Huai Army coordinated with Ever Victorious Army to fight a united front against Taiping Rebels. Between April and June 1863, the united front captured city by city and pushed the frontline to Kunshan. By August, Ever

Victorious Army attacked Suzhou. However, Taiping Rebels defended Suzhou heavily. For several months, Ever Victorious Army suffered heavy causality with no success.

Gordon obtained intelligence from his informant that one of the generals of the Taiping Rebels defending Suzhou, Gao Yong Kuan, had serious clash with the other commander Tang Shao Guang. Gordon suggested to Li to persuade Gao to surrender. When Li agreed, Gordon contacted Gao clandestinely. After Gao securing the guarantee of his own safety and the safety of his family and his staffs, he agreed to assassinate the other commander Tang. On December 4 1862, Gao killed Tang and surrendered. The Huai Army and Ever Victorious Army marched into Suzhou without firing a single shot.

By May 1864, the united front of Huai Army and Ever Victorious Army took Changzhou, midway between Shanghai and Taiping Rebels' capital Nanjing. Changzhou was the last important bastion of Taiping Rebels in the east front. The fall of Changzhou meant the days of Taiping Rebels were numbered.

During the campaign, Li expanded the Huai Army by absorbing the surrendered Taiping Rebels. After Li took Changzhou, he felt that the Huai Army was strong enough that he did not need Ever Victorious Army anymore. He asked Gordon to dissolve it. When Gordon agreed, Huai Army merged the Ever Victorious Army.

In order to appreciate the contribution from Ever Victorious Army, Li set up a monument in Shanghai to remember it. The monument is located in the Bund Garden today. It engraved the names of the forty-eight western commanders and soldiers sacrificed, lead by Frederick Townsend Ward. It is therefore also known as the Ward Monument.

When Li was ready to attack the stronghold of Taiping Rebels -Nanjing, the Huai Army were already 70,000 men strong.

Meanwhile, Taiping Rebels also lost ground in the west side to Xiang Army led by Zeng Guo Fan. It was under attack from both east and west fronts.

Finally, on May 15, 1864, Xiang Army and Huai Army jointly launched a major offense against Nanjing. Taiping Rebels leader Hong Xiu Quan had died in June. In July, Zeng took Nanjing, captured and executed all the remnants of Taiping Rebels and started three days of slaughter in the city, killing more than 100,000 civilians. Thus, fourteen years of Taiping

Rebellion ended. It was the most brutal civil war in the Chinese history. Nearly sixty million people perished directly and indirectly. China was exhausted. It also weakened Qing Dynasty both economically and politically.

Li's success in the Huai Army started his forty years of powerful political career. He was conferred the title of Count Suyi by the Qing Court, one of the highest title given to Han. Qing Court promoted him multiple times, initially as Viceroys of several provinces and later, to serve in the Capital to participate in making the decisions of key foreign affairs, economics, and military policies.

After the end of Taiping Rebellion, Zeng voluntarily dissolved his Xiang Army in order to avoid the jealousy and suspicion of the Qing Court. However, Li had a different view. He thought that it was not easy to establish an army and the country was still facing tremendous challenges from within and without. His army could be useful later.

While when Taiping Rebellion was rampant in the central China, Nian Rebellion was raging in the north. In 1865, Qing Court's Mongolian commander Sengelinqin, responsible for putting down the rebellion, suffered a major defeat. Qing Court ordained Zeng and Li to pacify the Nian Rebellion. However, since Zeng had already dissolved the Xiang Army, he borrowed Huai Army to launch the campaign. Li grouped 60,000 soldiers for him.

However, Zeng could not effectively command Huai Army. The campaign launched by Zeng was not successful. By late 1866, Qing Court finally decided to let Li do the job. Qing Court asked Zeng to return to his post as the Viceroy of Liangjiang, which included three provinces in central China.

Li effectively took control of Huai Army again and exterminated Nian Rebellion by the end of 1866. In the years to come, Li was ordained to put down the rebellions here and there, including the Miao minority uprising in the south, Muslim uprising in the west, and to solve the crisis with Western Powers in Tianjin.

Finally, Li became the Viceroy of Zhili and Minster of Commerce in Beiyang. He remained in the post for the next twenty-five years. He participated in the making the core decisions of politics, economics, foreign affairs, and military of the Qing Court. His Huai Army became the regular national army, stationed in different parts of the country, mostly along the coastlines, including Zhili, Shandong, Jiangsu, Guangdong, and Taiwan.

Li, the Industrialist

Different from the bureaucrats in the Qing Court, from early time on, Li showed candid interest in the Western technology. During his years of interface with foreigners, he profoundly felt that China needed a fundamental change. Wherever within his reach, he borrowed the concept from the West and implemented locally.

Initially, he purchased arms for Huai Army from foreigners. However, soon he established his own arm factory. In 1862, Li employed Englishman MaCartney Halliday, Gordon's friend, to be in charge of the arm factory, named Western Cannon Bureau. It was China's first Western weaponry factory. Soon, one factory expanded into three factories. Li also purchased an American owned ironworks in Shanghai to integrate vertically the weapon manufacturing business by providing the iron needed for the weapon production from his own factory. Later, Li moved its headquarter to Nanjing and renamed it as the Jinlin Manufacturing Bureau. Jinlin Manufacturing Bureau expanded rapidly. From the founding of 400 employees, it quickly increased to 1,200 employees, while MaCartney Halliday was in charge of the operation. He became one of the Li's most trusted subordinates.

Ironically, MaCartney married the daughter of the surrendered Taiping Rebels Gao Yong Kuan, who was executed by Li after his surrender. MaCartney returned to London working for the Chinese Embassy in 1874.

In 1869, when Li was the Viceroy of Zhili, the province with capital in Tianjin, he founded another weaponry factory modeled after Jinlin Manufacturing Bureau. He was credited as the father of Chinese modern weaponry industry.

In 1875, he had founded the largest Chinese private company -Zhao Shang Shipping Company. It was also the first Chinese company with shareholders. The founding of Zhao Shang Shipping Company also established a new business model, which had not existed in China before - the government organized private or public business. Even today, it is the most prevalent business model in China.

In seventies and eighties, Li has founded many enterprises -Hepei Coal and Iron Mining Company, Jiangxi Coal Mine Company, Hupei Coal Mine Company, Kaiping Coal Mine Company, Shanghai Machine Textile Company, Shandong Feng County Coal Mine Company, Tianjin Telegraph

Bureau, Shanghai Telegraph Bureau, Jingu Railroad Company, Tangxu Railroad Company, among many others. Suddenly, the modern industry started to flourish in China. It established the foundation of capitalism in China.

Tianjin Church Incident

July 1871, the church incident in Tianjin, created international news headlines. If not well handled, it could well be developing into another foreign power invasion that China could barely afford after two decades of civil strife.

In 1858, when China lost the "Second Opium War," Qing Court was forced to sign separate unequal treaties with England, France, Russia and the United States -the Tianjin Treaty. Among many other clauses, by which China lost many sovereign rights, one of them was that China would allow the freedom of preaching of Christian religions. Few years later, a French Catholic priest Jean Joseph Léon Talmier secured a piece of land in Tianjin to build a Catholic clinic. In 1869, the clinic built a church next to it. The church also provided shelters to many orphans. It was the first Catholic Church in Tianjin.

Figure 5 Tianjin Church Incident location

April and May 1870, there were several child-kidnap cases in Tianjin. When the city security guard caught the kidnaper Wu Lan Zeng, he claimed that he had sold the children to the church. However, the priests in the church denied. The event made an unexpected turn for the worse. Unfortunately, June that year, a plague was prevalent in Tianjin. Many orphans in the church died. The church workers wrapped up bodies in straw sheets and threw them to the backyard. Wild dogs fed themselves on the bodies. The scene horrified neighbors. Immediately, rumors spread that the priests were kidnapping children and took their organs to make medicine. It did not matter that it was not true. The mistrust was engulfing, and people were ready to believe in anything. The invasion of 1858, which killed many civilians, was still fresh in people's mind.

On June 21, the Magistrate Liu Jie took the kidnapper, Wu Lan Zeng, to the church to testify. Thousands demonstrator already gathered in front of the church. Demonstrator's emotion was running high, with banners demanding the justice, and thundering shouting from the crowd. When French consulate Henry Fontanie arrived in church with his guard Simon, the situation became confrontational. The multitude could no longer contain its sentiment. The uproar of multitude frightened Simon. When the security guards could no longer hold back the pressing crowds, he fired a shot and killed one of Magistrate Liu's servants. The demonstrators went wild. Immediately, the demonstrators invaded the church. The anger and resentment of the crowd were out of control. They vented their anger on anything in their way.

At the end of the day, the multitude killed Henry Fontanie, Simon and other ten priests and church workers, and burned down the church. The event was known as the Tianjin Church Incident.

Soon, France demanded retaliation. Qing Court asked the then Viceroy of Zhili, Zeng Guo Fan, to negotiate with French. The sentiment in the Qing Court also went high. Many officers wanted to prepare for the war. However, Zeng knew better. China could not afford another invasion. In the end, Zeng agreed to pay the compensation and prosecute the offenders. Twenty major offenders were sentenced to die. Fortunately, soon France was involved in the Franco-Prussian War, and did not have the extra attention to pursue this matter further.

The humiliating condition accepted by Zeng earned him dissatisfaction all over China, inside and outside of Qing Court. The event greatly damaged his reputation. One year later, he died at the age of sixty-three. Unfortunately, Li Hong Zhang would follow exactly his steps.

Beiyang Fleet

After Zeng passed away, Qing Court promoted Li to Zeng's positions and relied on Li for the general affairs of the country.

During the following years, excursions with foreign powers were frequent. In 1874, Japan invaded Taiwan. Luckily, Li was prepared. He dispatched Huai Army stationed in Xuzhou to defend Taiwan. He successfully fended off the Japanese. However, this would not stop Japan's ambition. Not much later, in 1880, Japan annexed Liuqiu, which was later known as Ryukyuan Okinawa.

In 1875, British troop entered Yunnan from Burma and killed the resisting Chinese. In the exchange of fire, Chinese defending force killed some British soldiers. Britain used this as an excuse to force China to sign the Yantan Unequal Treaty, in which China agreed to open additional ports for trade and British settlement and to allow British to enter Tibet. Since then British started the subversive activities in Tibet.

In 1883, France invaded Vietnam. The invasion lasted from December 1883 to April 1885. Both China and France won and lost some battles. In the Qing Court, the debates were also going on - Hawk faction vs. Dove faction. When the war became stalemate, Qing Court lost the will to fight. It asked Li to negotiate a peace. China conceded the right of protection of Vietnam. In effect, France colonized Vietnam. The treaty created outcry in China. It was said that "France won by not winning and China lost by not losing."

The public branded Li, by signing the unequal treaties and giving up much Chinese sovereignty right, as traitor. However, there was no doubt that he suffered to do so. He negotiated without any backup militarily or politically to take a strong position. Any impulsive decision would only invite more humiliation and concessions later. Li deeply realized that without catching up with the West in technology and economics, China was swimming against the tide.

By late nineteenth century, it was clear to Li that most of the threats on China came from the coast. Without a strong navy, it was impossible to defend the long coastline. Anywhere along the coastline was vulnerable. Many of the provinces along the coast were simply indefensible. Therefore, he became an aggressive proponent to establish a modern navy.

In 1874, he officially submitted his proposal to establish three navy fleets -Beiyang (North Sea), Dongyang (East Sea) and Nanyang (South Sea). At his urge, Qing Court started to build navy. The modern Chinese navy was born. Li also proposed to set up a second defense line on the land to augment the sea defense.

After the 1883 Sino-France War, when French navy annihilated the nascent Fujian Fleet, Qing Court decided to invest heavily to build up the navy. In 1885, Qing Court established a navy department. Emperor GuangXu's father, Prince Chunqing, became the Minister of Navy.

Li led the effort to build the largest of the three fleets –the Beiyang Fleet. Qing Court officially formed the Beiyang Fleet on December 17, 1888, by regrouping some existing and fragmented navy fleets. After the regrouping, Beiyang Fleet had 25 warships. The international press considered it the most powerful navy in Asia.

At the same time, Li wanted to move quickly to build the navy ports in Port Arthur, Dagu, and Weihai along the northern coast of China as his land defense strategy.

However, due to the budget constrain, Qing Court could not, or would not provide all the money needed to furnish a strong navy. Li had to compete with the project of Empress CiXi's royal garden for the budget. Any suggestion for holding the navy budget from CiXi' s Yihe Garden project was greeted as lack of respect of Empress CiXi. Certainly, it would cause CiXi' s displeasure. Li could not finish many implementations required.

Shortly, Li's effort was under a major test. The crippled Beiyang Fleet due to the shortage of budget was not a match against the Japanese fleet. In contrast, Japanese Emperor Meiji denoted his personal assets to fill the budgetary gap necessary for building the Japanese Navy. The event turned out to be a disaster for Qing Court. Eventually, Qing Court paid a price to Japan, which could build many Yihe Gardens.

Yihe Garden

One day, CiXi returned from an outing in Three Seas Royal Garden (ZhongHai, NanHai, BeiHai) next to the Forbidden City, she sighed: "How much I miss the old time when I had outing with the late Emperor XianFeng (CiXi's husband) in the Yuanming Garden. The Three Seas Royal Garden is good, but it is no comparison to the Yuanming Garden" .

When CiXi was saying it, she dropped tears. The palace servants were nervous and tried to comfort CiXi. The head of eunuch, Li Lian Ying, was next to CiXi, and an idea came to him.

Next day, Li Lian Ying went to the Grand Council and discussed with staff to see whether it was possible to restore Yuanming Garden. Staffs hesitated: "It will cost a lot of money to restore Yuanming Garden."

Yuanming Garden is located in the northwest suburb of Beijing. Qing Court started to build Yuanming Garden as a royal garden in 1709. Yuanming Garden and its neighboring gardens encompassed an area of more than hundred acres. The complex of royal gardens includes Three Mountains and Five Gardens. The three mountains are Wenzhou, Fuqua and Xiang. The five gardens are Wanchun, Yuanming, Changchun, Jinxing and Tingyi. Because the Yuanming Garden was the most famous one, the Royal Garden complex was known as Yuanming Garden.

During the subsequent emperors, Qing Court added many buildings and landscapes. It contained the best architects and artifact in China as built and collected by Qing Court over the one hundred and fifty years. British and French troops destroyed, looted, and burned down all just in couple of days during the Second Opium War.

One of the staffs commented, "It is not only expensive to restore the Yuanming Garden, but even if it were restored, Ex-emperor XianFeng is no longer there. I am afraid that Empress CiXi would feel sorry to be in the garden with only memories. Why not build a new garden instead?" Everybody thought it was a good idea.

When the staffs were discussing in succession, Prince Chunqing, Emperor GuangXu's real father, interjected: "Empress CiXi's birthday is coming in five years. It will be the right timing to build the garden and present to CiXi as gift for her birthday of the sixty years. Five years should be sufficient to build a garden."

Everybody agreed unanimously. Prince Chunqing frowned and continued, "But, where is the money coming from?" All pondered in silence.

Suddenly, Li Lian Ying clapped hands, "I got it. Didn't you set aside a budget for the navy every year 200 million tales of silver? Now it must be over 1 billion tales. China is a land-based country, why we need navy. Who would say no to use this money to build a garden for CiXi? She is the supreme ruler of China. If it is still not enough, we can ask for donation from rich people. For every seven thousand taels of silver anyone donates, we issue them an honorable title and a government position."

Figure 6 Yoshino battleship

Again, everybody concurred. Immediately, they drafted the edict to move the motion into action. When Li Lian Ying reported to CiXi about the plan, she did not say much, but was quite delighted in her heart.

Within months, hundred thousands of taels of silver were collected from the private donation in the name of naval defense. Previously, the private citizens could only achieve the government positions by years of study and passing the Imperial Literature Exam, now could buy the positions with money.

The result of donation was presented to CiXi. CiXi felt warmed, not so much by the money, but by the fact that people still bowed to her wishes. She asked Li Lian Ying to organize for the design and construction of the Yihe Garden.

Embezzlement

Li Hong Zhang's Beiyang Fleet consisted of two heavy weight battleships, over 7,000 tons, manufactured by Germany, two battle cruisers, over 3,000 tons, two cruisers, over 2,300 tons, four destroyers of various sizes, all capable of cruising at 16 knots. In addition, it also had six small gunboats. The largest battleship required three hundred soldiers to operate. Li had purchased warships from England and Germany between 1882 and 1889. It had formidable fighting power.

After 1890, the Qing Court cut the budget for the Beiyang Fleet due to the construction of Yihe Garden. It prevented Beiyang Fleet from buying more warships. However, the technology for warship evolved rapidly, especially in the maneuver speed and firepower. While Li could not pay for the order of a most advanced warship built by Britain due to the shortage of fund, Japan quickly grabbed it, and named it as Yoshino. It was capable of 22 knots of cruising speed, much faster than the best battleships of Beiyang Fleet, at 16 knots. Yoshino and other Japanese warships were also equipped with a type of cannons that fired projectiles at high speed, and low angles with a high rate of fire, five to six rounds per minute.

To fight for the budget was not Li's only problem of Beiyang Fleet. The Beiyang Fleet was also involved in smuggling and embezzlement. It caught Li's attention late in the game. Li staffed his fleet with most of his trusted subordinates from Huai Army. They thought that they were untouchable.

One of the commanders, Huang Rei Lan, embezzled the fund for ammunition for his personal use, and filled the arsenal with wooden boxes containing stones as camouflage. Li had long heard that his Beiyang Fleet was involving in smuggling. He decided to inspect the Fleet without advanced notice. During the inspection, not only he uncovered the case of smuggling, gambling, most unexpectedly, Li accidentally discovered the camouflaged arsenal boxes. Li was outraged, and immediately executed the commander.

However, the damage was beyond repair. Li could not replenish the shortage in arsenal in short order both for the lack of fund and for the lack of time.

Li decided to cover it up, because it would seriously discredit him to the outside world, especially to the Qing Court. He could only pray that there would be no war until he could make up the shortage of arsenal. However, the event turned out not so lucky for him. Soon, the Japanese started another invasion to Korea. It evolved into a nightmare to the Beiyang Fleet during Jiawu Sino-Japanese War. Japanese sank several of Beiyang warships when they ran out of the ammunition at the most critical moment of the battle.

Sino Japanese War

In 1894, Korea had another insurrection outbreak, the Tonghak Rebellion. Again, the Korean government asked Qing Court to support. At that time, Yuan Shi Kai was the Chinese Ambassador to Korea. China sent 2,500 soldiers to Korea around June 6 under the command of Yuan Shi Kai. He put down the Tonghak Rebellion successfully by June 11.

While the Chinese troop was ready to withdraw, Japan seized the opportunity, and landed 4,500 soldiers in Incheon, with additional reinforcement to arrive shortly. Chinese troop was outnumbered.

Li realized that the problem grew worse. In order to avoid an all-out war with Japan, as he was afraid of, Li asked British and Russia to intermediate. While Yuan was successful in putting down the rebellion, he was also strong proponent of fighting the war against Japan. Li Hong Zhang was concerned that he might aggravate the already very critical situation; he recalled Yuan back to China in late June. However, this time, Japan was well prepared, and was determined to escalate the event. The mediation failed on July 7, 1894.

After the mediation broke down, General Yoshimasa led Japanese brigades numbering about 4,000 marching from south of Seoul toward Asan Bay to face 3,500 Chinese troops garrisoned at Seonghwan Station east of Asan and Kongju. In response, Li had no choice but to dispatch more troops to Korea. Japan responded by further increasing its force in Korea to 8,000 strong. The tension escalated. The war was inevitable.

Figure 7 Sino Japanese War

By July 23, Japan moved in to occupy Seoul, seized the emperor and killed the Queen Min. Queen Min's end came rather dramatically and sadly. Because of her pro-China stance, Japanese considered her as obstacle. Several Japanese agents, under the order of Japanese Minister in Korea, Miura Goro, intruded into her palace, sized her, and burned her to death.

Queen Min was a very beautiful woman. She was also a progressive leader. She was very much devoted to the modernization of Korea. She had introduced modern education system. For the first time in history, Korea girls could be educated. She also welcomed missionaries, who had contributed much to the development of Western education. The arrival of an American medical missionary named Horace Newton Allen by the invitation of Queen Min in September 1884 also helped the rapid spreading of Christianity in Korea. She also made progress in the areas of press, economics, and military. It was a sad episode of Korean history. Japan immediately set up a puppet government consisting of the royal members entirely from the pro-Japanese faction.

After the fall of Seoul to Japanese hands, two forces encountered each other outside Asan in an engagement that lasted two days. The Chinese gradually lost ground to the superior Japanese numbers, and finally broke and fled towards Pyongyang, which is 100 miles north of Seoul.

There were 17,000 Chinese soldiers stationed in Pyongyang against 16,000 Japanese soldiers. The forces on both sides were about equal. When the two forces engaged outside of Pyongyang on July 28, the war became official. Both sides simultaneously declared the war on August 1.

In Pyongyang, the war was fought in three battlefields. While the battles were raging, the Qing commander in one of the battlefields, Ye Zhi Chao, made a fatal mistake to retreat. With one bastion open, the Chinese defense line became fragmented. Soon the tide was turned against Chinese army. Japanese Army surrounded Chinese army in the other two battlefields. On August 16, Chinese army was utterly defeated after several days and nights of intensive fighting. The other Chinese commander Zuo Bao Guei was killed in action.

By September, the remaining Chinese army retreated to the Korean-Chinese boarder -the Yulu River, further one hundred miles north of Pyongyang, with Japanese Army pursuing closely behind. China lost the land battle against Japan. Later, Commander Ye was prosecuted as a deserter. He barely escaped execution only at the Li's intervention.

In the sea front, on June 23, when the mediation was still in progress, Japan attacked and sank a Chinese warship "Gaosheng" outside of Incheon without prior notice, which was to become the trademark of Japanese military strategy. The actual sea battle did not happen until two months after Pyongyang fell to Japanese hand, when Beiyang Fleet encountered Japanese fleet in the Yellow Sea.

On September 17, eighteen of the warships of Beiyang Fleet faced the twelve Japanese warships outside the mouth of Yalu River. The commander of Beiyang Fleet, Ding Ru Can, was diffident of the fact that the fleet did not carry enough ammunition. He tried to avoid the head-on confrontation. However, it was not up to him how to engage the sea battle.

Although, Beiyang Fleet had more warships, but Japanese fleet had many more cannons. The Japanese cannons were also superior in accuracy and in firing rate, which was estimated six-time faster to the best Beiyang's cannons. In addition, the warships of Japanese fleet also had much faster cruising speed than Beiyang warships, not to mention that Beiyang Fleet was also crippled by its limited ammunition supply.

As an added misfortune, the commander of the fleet Ding Ru Can was badly hurt at the very onset of the battle not by enemy's fire, but by the explosion of its own cannon barrel. It showed how bad were the maintenance of Beiyang Fleet's equipment and the training of its soldiers. As Ding was unable to command the battle, the Beiyang Fleet effectively became leaderless. It discouraged the Chinese morale.

In the early afternoon, Japanese warships hit two Beiyang warships and sank one of them. On the other hand, Yoshino warship quickly recovered the damages from a wound.

Nevertheless, Beiyang Fleet was not defenseless. Its flagships, Dingyuan, Laiyuan and Jinyuan, inflicted serious damages on three Japanese ships.

When another Beiyang flagship, Zhiyuan, caught fire, while was combating Yoshino warship face-to-face, the captain, Deng Shi Chang, ordered the ship to commit a suicidal mission, to crash into Yoshino by marching at full speed toward it. Crews in Yoshino were horrified and aimed full firepower at Zhiyuan. Yoshino sank Zhiyuan before it could crash into Yoshino. All two hundred and fifteen crewmembers in Zhiyuan sank with the ship, including the captain.

Warship Jinyuan continued to fight Yoshino, but when it ran out of ammunition, it was also sunk. Two hundred fifty four crewmembers died.

Warships Dingyuan, Laiyuan and Zhenyuan, all catching fire, were seriously damaged. By late afternoon, when Japanese flagship Matsushima was hit and exploded, Japanese commander Ito Sukeyuki called to quit. Five hours of brutal battle was over.

At the end of the day, Beiyang Fleet lost five warships and over thousand soldiers died. Japanese fleet lost two warships and three others were badly damaged, including Yoshino warship.

There were multiple reasons for the defeat of Beiyang Fleet: Beiyang Fleet was inferior in weaponry and maneuver speed of its warships and lack of ammunition. In addition, from the very beginning, when the commander Ding was hurt, he lost the ability to command. The fleet became badly coordinated. Chinese fleet was entirely passive, only responding to Japanese attack.

The Last Days of An Empire

While China lost the war in Korea and in the sea, it was not the end of Jiawu Sino-Japanese War. Japan would not be content to occupy only Korea. Japan's ambition was to occupy China. Japan wanted to follow up the victory and invade China.

After the arrival of more reinforcements by the 10 October, Japanese repositioned their troop in Korea to launch another major offence, this time, into Chinese territory for the first time. On the night of October 24, 1894, Japanese successfully crossed Yalu River into Chinese territory undetected. Next day, they assaulted the outpost of Hushan, east of Jiuliancheng. China was completely unprepared that the war would spread into Chinese territory. The defenders deserted their positions; Jiuliancheng fell into Japanese hands without firing a shot. Soon General Yamagata's troop occupied the nearby city of Dandong. The Japanese had established a firm foothold on Chinese territory with almost no loss.

The easy success encouraged Japanese. The Japanese troop then split into two groups with one group advancing toward the city of Mukden, also known as Shenyang, and the other group pursuing the fleeing Chinese forces west toward the Liaodong Peninsula. By December 3, this group had captured the six towns in Liaodong Peninsula.

Meanwhile, Japan dispatched more troops from Japan under Commander Oyama Iwao by sea and landed on the south coast of Liaodong Peninsula on October 24. This troop, with 25,000 soldiers, was by far the largest troop in the conflict between China and Japan. Oyama's troop quickly moved to capture Jinzhou. On November 7, the Japanese prepared the siege to the strategic port of Port Arthur, or Dalian.

After two weeks of intense battle, by November 21, 1894, the Japanese occupied Port Arthur, and massacred thousands of Chinese civilians in an incident known as the Port Arthur Massacre. This was the beginning of fifty years of continuous Japanese aggression in China, which only ended in 1945 at the end of World War II.

For thousands of years, Japan revered China as her source of culture and civilization. It was the ultimate euphoria for Japanese to be able to feel superior toward China. It was a liberating experience. In the end, it costed both countries dearly.

Bohai Bay is a large bay outside of port Tianjin. The bay is like a crab with two claws folding inwards. The two claws are Liaodong Peninsula in the north and Shandong Peninsula in the south. Port Arthur is at the tip of

Liaodong Peninsula, and Weihaiwei is at the tip of Shandong Peninsula. By occupying both Port Arthur and Weihaiwei, Japan could cut off any sea route out of Tianjin port. Northern China would be defenseless from the attack from the sea. This was exactly what Japan intended to do.

After the defeat of battle at sea, the Chinese fleet subsequently retreated behind the Weihaiwei fortifications. On January 20, 1895, Japan launched assault on Weihaiwei. This was phase three of the Jiawu Sino-Japanese War. At that time, Beiyang Fleet still had twenty plus warships in Weihaiwei. However, Japan reinforced its troop to 25,000 soldiers under General Oyama Iwao's command, who had conducted a successful campaign in the Liaodong Peninsula. The troop landed in a remote coast of the east-most tip of the Shandong Peninsula.

On January 30, 1895, Oyama launched the attack of a forte south side of Weihaiwei. Qing's army had only three thousand soldiers. The commander, Zhou Jia En, defended to the end, inflicted heavy causality on the Japanese side, and killed a Japanese general Otera Yasusumi. On February 3, Japan took Weihaiwei.

When Japanese occupied Weihaiwei, Liugon Island, a small offshore island, where the base of Beiyang Fleet was located, became isolated. Japanese commander Ito sent a request to Ding Ru Cao to surrender, he flatly refused. On February 5, Japanese hit and stranded the Warship Dingyuan. Dingyuan continued to fire shots, until it exhausted the ammunition. Captain Liu Bu Chan committed suicide. Beiyang Fleet commander Ding also killed himself on 11 of February. Rest of the crewmembers sent a letter of surrender pretending to be from Ding to the Japanese. On 17 of February, Japanese landed on Liugon Island and took over all the possessions, including the remaining warships of the Beiyang fleet. By then, the Japanese had completed annihilated the Beiyang Fleet. It was a major setback for China. All the effort of building the navy went down the drain.

Earlier on the land, Qing Court appointed the Viceroy of Jiangsu and Jiangxi Provinces, Liu Kun Yi, reinforced by two generals Wu Da Deng and Song Qing Wei, to lead the task force to recover from the adverse condition. From January 17 on, Qing army attempted four attacks without success. Japanese Army was able to advance in several fronts, took cities like Senzhuang, Yingkou, Tianzhuangtai on the way.

The rapid advance of Japanese put Qing Court in panic. On February 18, 1895, Qing Court appointed Li Hong Zhang to negotiate with the Japanese.

However, the task was not easy. China was still losing battles day by day. By February 28, Qing army, 60,000 soldiers strong, had lost all the strongholds east of Liao River. Li had nothing in his hand that he could use as advantage to negotiate.

Figure 8 The signing of Maguan Treaty

When Li was in Japan for the negotiation, an assassin made an attempt on his life. The news made headlines worldwide. Li was only slightly hurt, but badly shaken. When he recovered and returned to the negotiation table on March 16, Japanese, under the pressure of international opinion, refrained from making further demands.

During the negotiation, Japanese forces opened another battlefield. It attacked the Pescadores Islands off the west coast of Taiwan. In a brief and almost bloodless campaign, the Japanese defeated the islands' Qing garrison and occupied the main town of Magong. This was another stroke of Japanese to get what she wanted. Without spending effort, Japan put another piece of prey on the negotiation table.

When China and Japan finally signed the treaty on March 23, 1895, China agreed to pay an indemnity of 200 million silver taels, which was many times larger than the Japanese annual government budget at that time. Japan also took control of Liaodong Peninsula, southern half the Manchuria, took possession of Taiwan and Pescadores Island. The newly captured warships from Beiyang Fleet and the war compensation from China allowed Japan to strengthen their Navy tremendously, which eventually paved the way for the defeat of Russian Second Pacific Squadron ten years later. In addition, China agreed Japan to be the protector of Korea, in essence, Japan's right to colonize Korea. It was known as the Maguan Treaty, or the Treaty of Shimonoseki in Japanese.

After the signing of Maguan Treaty, Russia, Germany, and France felt that their interests in China were threatened by Japan; they jointly forced Japan to give up the concession of Liaodong in a deal called the Triple Intervention. Under pressure, Japan reluctantly agreed to give up Liaodong Peninsula, not free but to extort more money out of China, an additional 30 million taels of silver. Much to Japan's astonishment and consternation, Russia moved almost immediately to occupy the entire Liaodong Peninsula and especially to fortify Port Arthur. Russian's move sowed the seed of Russo-Japanese War. Meanwhile, the fight to secure interests in China by foreign powers intensified.

The signing of Maguan Treaty created a commotion in China. The public media heavily denounced Li Hong Zhang. Qing Court was under pressure to relieve all of Li's government posts temporarily, including the Viceroy of Zhili, a post he had held for the past twenty-five years in order to pacify the dissidents. Li also swore that he would not negotiate any more treaties for the Qing Court.

It also signified the failure of all reforms so far. It opened another page in the Chinese history -the emergence of school of thoughts of more drastic reform. It also paved the way for the Wuxu coup, sponsored by Emperor GuangXu himself against the wish of Empress CiXi.

Spoiled Birthday

CiXi's sixtieth birthday was October 10, 1894. The preparation for a grand celebration started more than a year ago. CiXi wanted to imitate the grand style of the fourth and the greatest emperor of Qing – QianLong in eighteenth century. QianLong expanded Qing Dynasty to its height. During his sixty-year reign, he had conquered much of the Chinese west and shaped Qing into a prosperous nation. Several generations of emperors enjoyed the fortune created by him until the end of Qing, when the country was finally exhausted. He died at an age of eighty-eight. In his old ages, QianLong went into a spending spree at old age; he built the luxurious Yuanming Garden. He held the procession miles long for his birthday party.

CiXi envied him. She also had a birthday party plan for herself. On her birthday, she would receive the congratulation of the court officials and delegates all over the country in the Forbidden City, then to set off the royal procession with her chariot escorted by hundreds of eunuchs and court servants, departing the Forbidden City from Xihua Gate, and going to Yihe Garden. There would be decorated flags, archways, altars for the chanting of Buddhist monks, and platforms for Beijing operas to perform, on both sides of the road, which was about ten miles long, leading to Yihe Garden, which was ready for inauguration after a construction of stretching five-years long and costing hundreds millions tales of silver.

In Yihe Garden, she would set a state banquet for thousand guests. She was ready to show her proud garden to the nation. After the banquet, there would be her favorable opera shows. Everything followed the protocol of Emperor QianLong.

Inexpertly, while the preparation was going on briskly, Japan provoked the war in July. In October, the war was waging on intensely. Partly because CiXi misappropriated the funds for Beiyang Fleet to build her Yihe Garden, China lost the war.

To show her support for the navy symbolically, CiXi built a stone boat in the lake in the Yihe Garden. She wished that the Beiyang Fleet were unsinkable just like her stone boat in the lake.

The war disrupted CiXi's celebration plan. On September 25, she ordered the cancelation of all celebration programs. She spent a disheartened birthday in the Forbidden City.

Stage for Coup

During Li Hong Zhang's career, he negotiated and signed more than thirty unequal treaties for Qing Court. He had given up China's money, territory, and sovereign rights. Despite all the contribution had made, in Chinese history, he was not regarded positively. However, his hands were tied. Confucius teaching bounded him. He never thought to rebel. He worked within the framework he was allowed.

Qing Court was grateful to the intervention of Russia, Germany, and France to save Manchuria from Japan. At the request of Russia, Li Hong Zhang signed a Sino-Russo Secret Treaty. In this treaty, China agreed to let Russia to build railroad in Manchuria and in the event of Japan's aggression, Russia would help China to defend. By this agreement, Russia did not send one soldier, got the rights in Manchuria that Japan gave up.

After signing the treaty, he attended the coronation ceremony of Tsar Nicholas II on May 14 in Uspensky Cathedral. After leaving Russia, he took the chance to have a grand tour of Europe, witnessed firsthand the prosperity of Europe, its mighty industry, and received government reports from the host countries of their political systems. Upon returning to China, Li was totally convinced by the reform.

After his return, CiXi transferred him to be the Viceroy of Guangdong and Guangxi Provinces in the south of China, next to Hong Kong. Luckily, for him, he was away from Beijing when another catastrophe happened. This time, the Capital of China, Beijing, was occupied by the invading powers. Qing Court fled to the interior of China -Xian, a city one thousand mile to the southwest of Beijing.

However, before the Eight-Nation Alliance invasion, another earthshaking event happened. In 1898, Emperor launched a coup d'état. When it failed, Empress CiXi put Emperor GuangXu under house arrest.

The Last Days of An Empire

Chapter 3

Kang You Wei

In May 1895, after Qing Court signed the Maguan Treaty with Japan, public opinion in China was agitated. From south to north, people grouped together to condemn Qing Court and Li Hong Zhang. Kang You Wei was one of the most outspoken critics.

Kang was a student of Chinese Literature. After several failed attempts to pass the Imperial Literature Exam for pursuing a political career, he was very discouraged.

In 1891, when he was thirty-three years old, he returned to Guangdong, his home province. Guangdong at that time, due to the geographic proximity to Hong Kong, received heavy influence from the West. As Kang was looking for alternatives to pursue his dream, his exposure to the new ideas from the West gradually changed his belief.

He had read widely, comparing the Western ideas with his Confucius training, trying to make a sense out of the confusion. He read extensively the Western history, modern or ancient, world geography, the treatises of Gu Yen Wu, an important Chinese philosopher in the seventeenth century, and many others. He also realized that the reason China could not adapt Western systems for her use, whether political or economical, was due to the incompatibility of the logics between Chinese and Western way of thinking. To apply the Western systems in China, one needed to understand both in-depth, fully digest them, and sort out how to apply the Western system without causing the dislocation.

Zhang Zhi Dong, the contemporary with Li Hong Zhang, one of the four pillar administrators in late Qing, had a slogan: "Use Chinese system as the core to apply Western system in practice." Besides Li Hong Zhang, he was the other one who built up large-scale nascent industries in central China, most notable -Hanyan Iron Works, Daye Mining Company, Hanyang Arsenal, several railroads, among many others.

However, Kang was pondering, "Despite all these reforms employing the Western technologies, why Qing was getting weaker but not stronger? There must be something fundamentally wrong."

Kang then realized that the answer was the "system." In China, the Literature Exam system sucked the best minds of China. Thousands if not millions of young people dedicated nothing else but to study the ancient Confucius teaching: no science, no math, no technology, and no medicine, not to mention business, which was the lowest profession in China. The Confucius teaching was nothing but morale restraint to demand the obedience and loyalty: subjects loyal to emperors, students loyal to teachers, sons loyal to parents, wives loyal to husbands. It had been a tool used by the ruling class to exert control since two thousand years ago. He saw it not only the obstacle to his own career but also the hindrance to China progress.

Kang was a conceited person. He suffered humiliation when he could not pass the Literature Exam. He was determined to overthrow it.

At that time, it was popular to organize study groups. People participated in the study groups to express their view freely. Initially, he organized his study group in Guangdong. In 1895, Beijing was fervent after China lost the Jiawu Sino-Japanese War. He felt that he had to be in the place of action. He moved his study group to Beijing, and renamed it as "Power Study Association."

When China was defeated in the war, many strong-minded people were looking for a way to save the nation. Kang was not the only one. Study groups became popular as the brainstorming place. Kang's "Strong Study Association," advocating political reform through the publication of newspapers, soon attracted a lot of attention and adherence. The membership grew quickly. Soon, he branched out in Shanghai. The association gradually evolved into a political party, asserting certain reform agendas for the Qing Court.

What Kang did clearly stepped beyond the tolerance limit of Qing Court. His severe criticism of Li Hong Zhang also annoyed Li. Soon, Qing Court cracked down on Kang's associations. Overnight, Kang gained his fame nation-wide.

Kang achieved a breakthrough by writing a long proposal of reform addressed to Emperor GuangXu. Kang had published it before submitting to Emperor GuangXu. It received warm receptions from media. Kang formally submitted his proposal to Emperor GuangXu through a government branch office called the Discipline Inspection Institute on May 2, 1895. Thousands of similarly minded people endorsed the proposal.

Kang's proposal was only one of hundreds of petitions submitted to the Discipline Inspection Institute during that period, after the signing of Maguan Treaty. However, it was the most significant one. Few of these petitions actually arrived on the desk of the Emperor. Nevertheless, since GuangXu already heard about Kang, and was aware of his proposal through media, he insisted on seeing it despite the attempt to block the proposal from him by some court officers.

After GuangXu read it, he was swayed. The proposal was a comprehensive outline of the reform plan. Kang' s plan was not empty rhetoric, but full of details of execution. He was against the revolution. He thought that revolution was bloody, cited the example of French revolution. His plan was a peaceful, three-step implementation to achieve a constitutional monarchy. Kang's plan left a deep impression in GuangXu's mind. It further strengthened his intention to reform. However, GuangXu did not take action until 1898.

Wuxu Coup

Out of major European powers, only Germany had not gained any benefit in China, she was drooling. In November 1897, German priest George Stenz's confrontational behavior antagonized Chinese in a village in Shandong. In response, Chinese people stormed into his residence, and killed two priests while looking for George, who was not present. Germany found a good excuse and immediately occupied Qingdao, a major seaport on the Shandong Peninsula. The incident was resolved only after China signed another unequal treaty, to lease Qingdao for 99 years, to concede the railroad and mining rights in Shandong to Germany. It again triggered a nation-wide outcry.

Following the incident, while the nation was agitated over the treaty with Germany, Kang organized a new group called "Association of Protecting the Nation." Within a month, Kang recruited hundreds of members.

GuangXu had wanted to summon Kang for long time, but his staffs persuaded him not to do so. In early 1898, GuangXu could eliminate all the reluctance from his subordinates and summoned Kang.

During Kang's audience with GuangXu, he talked smoothly and eloquently about his plan. Kang was a proficient speaker. He could lead GuangXu's logic into his theories of reform. GuangXu was very convinced and delighted.

Figure 9 GuangXu (middle)

Since then, Kang was in and out of the palace often to see GuangXu. Kang firmly planted the seed of reform in GuangXu's mind. The two often talked long hours to map out strategy for execution.

Finally, on June 11, 1898, Emperor GuangXu sent an edict to the nation to announce his intention to reform. It immediately became the hottest headline. Inside the Qing Court, people were discussing, gossiping, and commenting. Something usual was about to happen and big cloud and storm were gathering.

Once the edict was out, Kang brought his disciples and his brother, Kang Guang Ren, into Qing Court to discuss reform with GuangXu.

Within the Qing Court, there were sympathizers of reformers, like Viceroy Zhang Zhi Dong, and there were officers who were loyal to Emperor GuangXu, like Emperor's private teacher, the Imperial Tutor, Weng Dong He, and court officer Yang Sen Xiou. Soon, GuangXu brought in the supporters for reform to participate in the discussion and planning.

In order to give Kang and his disciples' administration power, GuangXu conferred official positions and titles to Kang and his disciples. With the court positions, conferred titles, and most importantly, Emperor's support, the reformers were highly encouraged, buoyant and behaved as if they were the saviors of the nation.

As their influence and authority grew, their attitude drew resentment from the rest of the court. Many officers started to complain, grumble and to submit reports to CiXi that a group of fanatic scholars with treacherous ideologies dangerously misled Emperor GuangXu. If CiXi did not stop them, they would lead to the destruction of Qing Dynasty.

GuangXu, taking the advice from reformers, issued several edicts every day, as he had never done before. He was anxious to change the country. He wanted to complete the reform as soon as possible. Therefore, he made many changes forcefully, such as the changes involving reorganization in the Qing Court or the provincial governments. When cutting the government offices, some positions were eliminated, while new ones were created. The edicts met a lot of resistance obviously from those who suffered from the reform, both inside the court and in the provinces. Qing Court was Balkanized.

Many officers sent petitions to GuangXu to advise him retrieve his orders. It led to the dismissal of several highly influential officers.

The situation of reform became chaotic. GuangXu and the reformers simply did not have the means to follow up the orders through to the level of implementation. Local officials often ignored the orders, or worse, openly challenged them. Other orders were not practical because they did not fit the reality. Many edicts contradicted each other. Although the reformers had a good intention, but they did not have any administration experience, neither did GuangXu. Nor did they have enough political capital and apparatus in place for such large-scale reform.

One of the most drastic reforms was to abolish the thousand year's old Literature Exam system, which Kang failed miserably. Kang detested the system and vowed to destroy it. Kang's opportunity came. When GuangXu issued the edict to close down the Literature Exam once for all, the upheaval was more than overwhelming. The system had been the only way for commoners to achieve political careers in China for the last two thousands of years. The abolishment of the exam system meant the loss of the career path for millions who had dedicated themselves for their lifetime quest.

The reformers also openly advocated aligning with Japan and Britain to fend off Russia. While it attracted the sympathy from Japan and Britain, it alienated many people who distrust Britain and Japan in particular.

CiXi was increasingly uneasy about what GuangXu was doing. She had officially returned the power to GuangXu when GuangXu reached his adulthood several years ago. However, GuangXu's inexperience and naiveness worried her. GuangXu was not tactful in building consensus. He did not know how to exercise his power and was weak. Others could easily swing him.

One day, GuangXu went to see CiXi. CiXi said, "GuangXu, there are a lot of rumors about you, you know."

GuangXu replied nervously, "What kind of rumors?"

"For example, people said that you want to convert to Christian. I also heard that you want to cut your ponytail. I do not believe it; however, there are many people come to me to complain what you are doing. What do you say?"

GuangXu did not know where CiXi was leading to, but was both concerned and upset by the unfounded rumors, said hesitantly, "I was trying to do the best for the country. The rumors are not true."

CiXi ridiculed, "Now you become all capable, you don't have to come to see me anymore. But remember, be careful what you do, don't let those fanatics destroy what we have."

GuangXu felt quite uneasy and knew that the trouble was brewing. When GuangXu returned to his quarter, he told the unpleasant encounter to the Imperial Tutor, Weng Dong He. Weng contemplated: "CiXi's displeasure is most directly to Kang. With Kang in the court, he is more hindrance than help. Because CiXi thinks, Kang is behind everything you do. Why Your Highness does not send him away to appease CiXi? He can still work for you from outside."

GuangXu thought it was a good idea. He immediately discussed this idea with Kang. Kang reluctantly agreed. GuangXu asked Kang to go to Shanghai to create a newspaper to advocate the new reform.

The conflict soon escalated. CiXi's attitude toward GuangXu was also getting harsher. The reports to complain GuangXu's reform arrived at CiXi at increasing frequency and severity. GuangXu realized that eventually, CiXi would act and destroy everything he had accomplished.

One day, Yuan Shi Kai came to see him to report the status of Beiyang Army. Suddenly, an idea clicked in GuangXu's mind: "Never in the world can one achieve political change without the backup of military power..."

It was a dangerous thought. While Yuan was reporting, GuangXu's mind was elsewhere. He could not concentrate to listen what Yuan had to say. When Yuan finished reporting, and was about to leave, GuangXu suddenly asked, "You trained your army for so long. If one day, country needs their service, are you ready?"

Without suspecting GuangXu's intention, Yuan firmly replied, "Of course, Your Majesty, Beiyang Army belongs to you. It will be loyal to you forever."

GuangXu followed: "You see the situation in China is very critical. Without drastic reform, we are getting weaker every day. Foreign powers erode our sovereign day by day. I do not see any way out but to reform. Therefore, I have launched reform two months ago. However, there are many resistances, and what I could achieve is limited, because my hands are tied..."

Yuan was smart, immediately he realized what GuangXu was implying. GuangXu's unexpected turn started to fret him. However, he waited.

GuangXu realized that one more step ahead, he would pass the point of no return, but he could not stop now, neither did he want to: "I want you to disarm the Yihe Garden palace guards, and encircle the Garden until further notice. But you should do no harm to CiXi."

As if a thunder struck, he was speechless, and sweated out. It was Emperor GuangXu against Empress Dowager. It was a no win game with disastrous consequence for him.

GuangXu realized Yuan's difficulty; however, he could not take back what he just said, nor did he want to. He continued, "I don't want to do any harm to CiXi. I only want to make sure that those who are against reform will not disturb her with unfounded rumors and complain about me anymore. After this is over, I will reward you handsomely. "

After leaving GuangXu's quarter, Yuan analyzed the situation. GuangXu and his reformers was no match to CiXi and the conservative gang. The reformers were nothing but a bunch of idiot, inexperienced scholars. They had no power, no backup, just some empty talk. Even GuangXu was weak in front of CiXi. CiXi's wrath could easily subdue GuangXu. There was no way GuangXu could stand against CiXi. It was a suicidal mission to support GuangXu.

The next day, GuangXu again summoned Yuan to secure his commitment. Yuan was not able to say no to GuangXu. However, he had plotted out his own strategy.

When he returned to Tianjin, he went to visit Yong Lu, CiXi's cousin, and a loyal CiXi follower. He was the Commander of Capital Defense Force, which also included the Palace Guards.

After briefing Yong Lu what happened. Yong Lu said, "We should not take this lightly, before anything more serious happens."

Under Yong Lu's urge, two of them went to see CiXi. When they arrived in Yihe Garden, it was already very late at night. Yong Lu stressed the urgency of this matter, and CiXi received them. As expected, CiXi was outraged. She instructed Yong Lu to round up the reformers, Kang and his disciples.

Fortunately, Kang and Liang Qi Chao, one of his disciples, left Beijing the previous day for the new assignment in Shanghai, and escaped. Soon, they exiled to Japan. However, other reformers were not so lucky.

When Emperor heard that CiXi was returning to the Forbidden City, escorted by the Imperial Palace Guards, commanded by Yong Lu, GuangXu was in panic. He tried to inform reformers to flee, but it was too late. Yuan was nowhere to be seen.

Qing Court crushed the reform on September 21, 1898. It lasted exactly one hundred and three days. Therefore, it was known as the "Hundred Days Reform," or "Wuxu Coup" designated by the year 1898 in Chinese calendar as year of Wuxu.

Qing Court sentenced six leaders of the reformers, Kang's disciples and brother, to death and executed them within days on September 28. Other reformers were either imprisoned or exiled to the west frontier of China - Xinjiang. Kang himself managed to escape and went to exile in Japan.

GuangXu himself was under house arrest on a small island called Yantai in Nanhai Lake in the Imperial Park. He would never regain his freedom. This was neither his last mis-fortune. Qing Court claimed that GuangXu was sick. Both British and French ambassadors offered to send their doctors for GuangXu, but CiXi rejected. There was discussion, whether GuangXu should be deposed. CiXi started to look for a candidate. However, a suitable candidate did not come easily.

Western media, out of sympathy to GuangXu, further discredited CiXi. Empress Dowager CiXi detested their sympathy to GuangXu. It enhanced the mistrust between CiXi and foreign powers.

During his life-long house arrest, Emperor GuangXu spent most of his times working with watches and clocks, which had been a childhood fascination, as his pastime.

Heir Apparent

When GuangXu was under house arrest, the voices to depose him were incessant. Those voices were from the Princes, who had sons who could be the candidate for the future emperor. They were constantly soliciting CiXi to consider their sons as new emperor. The motivation was clear. Once the son was crowned as Emperor, the father would be Regent with all the power and prestige that followed.

The loudest voice was coming from Prince Duan, who was GuangXu's cousin. To add more of their royal blood, Prince Duan's wife was CiXi's niece, who was quite close to CiXi. His son, Fu Hui, was thirteen years old in 1898. Prince Duan was working feverishly on CiXi to confer Fu Hui as emperor. CiXi's confidant, Youg Lu, was also in favor. CiXi found that Fu Hui was slow-witted, easy to control. This was exactly the quality of an emperor that met CiXi's expectation.

In December 24, 1899, CiXi issued an edict to confer Fu Hui as the heir apparent to the throne. It would be followed by deposing GuangXu in January the following year, and then to crown Fu Hui officially as emperor.

Unexpectedly, resistance came from all directions. In the Qing Court, heavy weight officers, like Li Hong Zhang, Zhang Zhi Dong, and many others, jointly submitted their petitions to advise CiXi not to do so. They said that GuangXu had not done anything wrong, and should not be deposed. Domestically, the elites from Shanghai, including Chairman of the Shanghai Telegraph Company, Jin Yuan Shan, sent petition to CiXi endorsed by fifteen thousand people. In Hupei Province in Central China, a group consisting of fifty influential local scholars and businesspersons went to Beijing for petition. Foreign powers also exerted pressure -Britain, France, Japan, and Russia all issued warnings that they would refuse to recognize the new emperor. CiXi would not do anything to offend foreign powers. She scrapped the plan. Prince Duan was very upset because he had the most to lose. His wish and dream evaporated. The heart of revenge was born.

The Boxers

The Box Rebellion was the next major disaster afflicted on Qing Dynasty. This event struck a final nail in coffin of Qing Dynasty. The uprising took place in response to aggression of foreign power in China. The movement arose out of the anti-Western sentiment. Among ordinary Chinese, the Boxers enjoyed massive popular support. However, without Qing Court's encouragement and support, it would not become such a catastrophe.

On one hand, Qing Court resisted reform to strengthen China fundamentally. On the other hand, its anti-foreign sentiment continued to grow. When the Boxers came, as they claimed that they were impenetrable by bullets, the ignorant Qing Court looked upon as the way to expel foreign powers.

However, the Boxer Rebellion, sponsored by Qing Court, appalled many Chinese intellectuals and scholars. They called the Boxers "bandits."

Nevertheless, the incident exposed that the corrupted Qing Court was beyond salvation. It no longer behaved like a sensible government, rather like a prodigal son facing an inevitable ending.

By 1898, spurred on by state fiscal collapse and natural disasters, the Boxers emerged out of Shandong, violently targeting Christian missions. Initially, Qing Court suppressed them, who reminded Qing Court of the Nian Rebellion years ago.

The event made a drastic turn when Prince Duan realized that the Boxers were exactly what he needed to vent his hate on foreign evils.

Eight-Trigram is the symbol of the Book of Changes -The I Ching. For centuries, Chinese used I Ching as a living, breathing oracle. The Chinese believes it will help to promote success and good luck and to impart balance and perspective to the life. Various religious sects borrowed the Eight Trigram as their symbol to mystify. "Eight -Trigram Sect," founded by Liu Zuo Chen in early Qing Dynasty, was one of those religious sects. The cult was preaching a combination of Confucianism, Taoism, and Buddhism and its mystic power. It became popular in the mid eighteenth century. Later, when Wang Lun became the cult leader, he proclaimed that he was the emperor. Qing Court banned and suppressed it. The cult went underground, and changed names several times. It remained as a secret society, attracting some converts. Over the course of a century, there were several uprisings derived from the underground cult.

The Boxers, or in Chinese known as "The Society of Righteous and Harmonious" by literal translation, evolved from the Eight-Trigram Sect. The people, having lost their livelihoods due to foreign aggression and natural disasters, became its breeding ground. Westerners called them "Boxers" due to their martial art practice.

The Boxers' primary peculiarity was spirit possession, which involved the whirling of swords, violent prostrations, and chanting incantations. Under the spirit protection, the boxers claimed that they were invincible against guns and cannons.

The Boxer Rebellion arose from Zhang Luan, a born leader, his daughter, Zhang Xiu Ying and son-in-law Li Lai Zhong. After Germany occupied Qingdao, the Boxers raised the banner "Support Qing and Destroy Foreigners" to recruit members and preach the cult. Zhang had learned some tricks of medicine to cure disease. When he was treating the sick ones, he put up a show using the combination of talisman and curse. This added to his mystic nature by claiming his unique healing power.

When the wife of Shandong Viceroy, Yu Xian had dystocia, and the doctors were helpless, Yu Xian called in Zhang Luan for help. Miraculous, Zhang Luna delivered the baby successfully. Out of gratitude, Yu Xien offered money to Zhang. However, Zhang refused the money but requested the permission to preach his cult and protection in Shandong. The Viceroy was more than happy to comply.

Since then, Zhang Luan's cult activity was no longer clandestine. His fame grew so as his followers. Within a half year, his cult grew to nine thousand members. The daughter Zhang Xiu Ying proclaimed herself "the Saint." They dressed up in red and carried red lanterns roaming the land and causing perturbation and despair. They burned the churches and killed Chinese Christians.

The Viceroy Yu Xian himself was quite anti-Christian for a good reason. Due to the immunity and foreign power protection in the foreign concessions and churches, many criminals, prosecuted by the government, converted into Christians and hid inside churches, in order to receive protection. Churches, inevitably, became the shelters for criminals. Despite a lot of good work done by missionaries, churches were perceived as a place to hide criminals. It was another source of conflict between churches and general population. It gave Yu Xian further reason that he did not want to interfere Zhang Luan's anti-foreign activities.

In the winter of 1899, a British missionary was killed in Shandong. Due to the British protest, Qing Court demoted and transferred Yu Xian; it appointed Yuan Shi Kai to be the new Viceroy. Yuan saw the situation was out of control, and sent his army to put down Zhang Luan's cult. In combat, Zhang Luan was killed, but his daughter and son-in-law escaped. Since they could not stay in Shandong anymore, the couple led the remnants migrating to Tianjin.

This was after Li Hong Zhang's transfer to be the Viceroy of Guang-dong and Guangxi, as a result that he lost the Jiawu Sino-Japanese War and signed an unfavorable treaty. Prince Duan took over Li's position as the commander of the army. This was a fateful coincidence.

Since CiXi gave up his son as the heir apparent under the pressure, Prince Duan developed a hatred for foreigners. His anti-foreign rhetoric was a public knowledge. The Boxers thought they could get support from Prince Duan, and asked to see him. After the first meeting, the Boxers tactfully demonstrated their marshal art skills. They also demonstrated their ability to perform diviner and mystical ritual, which they claimed to be invincible against guns and cannons. Prince Duan was overjoyed. It did not matter whether he believed the magic curse or not. He thought he could use the Boxer to revenge against the foreigners. He christened the Boxer as "The Society of Righteous and Harmonious."

Soon, Prince Duan went to see CiXi to report about "The Society of Righteous and Harmonious." He claimed that how they were patriotic and capable of expelling foreigners. CiXi had her doubt: "I cannot believe that a group of untrained vagabonds can defeat the foreigners better than our troops."

Meanwhile, many Boxers moved into Beijing, preaching the cult and burning churches. Many missionaries and foreign civilians fled to their embassies for protection. Western Powers were alarmed, and protested to the Qing Court.

Conflict Began

Soon, the encounter became ugly. The German consul Clemens von Ketteler brutally attacked a Chinese civilian without provocation. The event agitated the anti-foreign sentiment. The Boxers and thousands of Chinese Muslim Gansu warriors, stationed near the Capital, under General Dong Fu Xiang of the Imperial Army went on a rampage against the Westerners. A Manchu Captain, En Hai, killed von Ketteler during the encounter. Japanese attaché Sugiyama Akira met the same fate in the street few days later. When Viceroy of Zhili, Yong Lu, heard the news, he was at a complete loss. He hurried to see CiXi.

At the same time, Prince Duan wanted deliberately to incite the disturbance, forged a warning letter from foreigners, saying that if Qing Court would not release Emperor GuangXu from house arrest, it would face a grave consequences. Upon seeing the letter, CiXi was infuriated.

Prince Duan took advantage of CiXi's rage, said, "Foreigners are stepping out of their boundaries. If we don't do something, I am afraid that, soon or later, they will intervene in our internal policies."

CiXi asked him in doubt, "What strategy do you have?"

Prince Duan took the opportunity, "I have interviewed the Boxers. They are truly patriot. Foreigners in Shandong destroyed their livelihood. They are asking the Court to defend our country. They are also experts in the martial arts, and they can fight well. I suggest we use them to fend off foreigners."

Yong Lu knew that it was Prince Duan's ploy, but since CiXi was furious about the letter, he dared not to say anything. Soon, Prince Duan secured CiXi's permission to use the Boxer as defense force. Prince Duan started to organize the Boxers to attack.

When other officers heard about the news, both Manchu and Han alike came to petition CiXi to reconsider. CiXi was still under rage, saying, "You only know how to take sides with foreigners. You do not know how they bully us."

Under Prince Duan's urge, anyone against the Boxer was severely punished. That was the end of discussion.

Prince Duan got a free hand to mobilize the Boxers. Soon, the opposition was quiet. Under Prince Duan's protection, the Boxers set up their headquarters in the Forbidden City, and built a high altar. People in the court were in awe to see the Boxers in and out of the Forbidden City.

Qing Armies

In Qing Dynasty, or in Chinese history, due to the extension of her territory, there was no national army. There were regional armies commanded by native generals and carried strong local elements. Xiang and Huai Armies were typical.

The Manchu Armies, also called the Eight Banner Armies, were the only Armies, which stationed throughout China, because Manchu was the ruling class. Other armies were regional.

In western China, where the Muslim influence was strong, the armies consisted of Muslim soldiers. Likewise, there were Mongol Armies. In the second half of the nineteenth century, Qing Court also allowed the formation of Han Armies, like Xiang and Huai Armies. The lately and newly formed Beiyang Army and Navy modeled after Western Armies consisted of mostly Han people.

When the conflict with foreigners arose in early 1900, there were three armies nearby Beijing under Qing Court disposition: the Eight Banner Army, the Imperial Chinese troops, which defended the Capital, and Muslim Army.

General Dong Fu Xiang, a Chinese Muslim, led the Muslin Army. In the Muslin Army, most of the soldiers were Chinese Muslim from the western provinces of China, such as Xinjiang, also known as the Chinese Turkistan, and Gansu Province, the starting point of the ancient Silk Road. In 1895-1896, Rebel Chinese Muslims and Turkic Salars had revolted. General Dong crushed the revolt successfully, and received merits from Qing Court. When the western frontier was peaceful, in 1898, Qing Court drafted Dong and his 10,000 men Muslim troops to Beijing to protect the capital against foreign invasion.

The Muslim troops were organized into eight battalions of infantry, two squadrons of cavalry, two brigades of artillery, and one company of engineers. The Muslim Gansu Braves were incorporated into the Capital Defense Force under the commander of Rong Lu. General Dong Fu Xiang, reporting to Rong Lu, became the Commander-In-Chief of all the Chinese armies near Beijing. They intimidated the Western forces. They were eager to join the Boxers and attack the foreigners.

Among the Han Armies, part of the Huai Army under the commander of General Nie also participated in the defense of Tianjin. He personally disliked the Boxers.

The Boxers were not an army. They were a group of disorganized mobs, although many of them might be motivated by patriotism. Others joined because of their anti-foreign sentiment. However, it was the wrong way to show patriotism. At the request of Prince Duan, Muslim Army under the Command of General Dong absorbed most of them into Muslim Army.

The other Qing Armies that Qing Court could dispose in a short notice were Yuan Shi Kai's Beiyang Army in Shandong, a neighboring province south of Zhili and the Eight Banner Armies in Manchuria. However, Yuan was reluctant to send his troop to help, since he was the one who crashed the Boxer at the very beginning. He saw the Boxers as rebels. The Eight Banner Army in Manchuria would soon be tied up to defend against Russian invasion.

Invasion

Throughout May 1900, as the situation became tense, the foreign navies started building up their presence along the northern China coast. Austria-Hungary, France, Germany, Italy, Japan, Russia, the United Kingdom and the United States jointly formed an Alliance.

The Alliance powers soon started to organize an expedition army. The force eventually totaled 45,000 soldiers, initially under the commander of Russian General Linevitch from the First Siberian Corp of Russian Imperial Army in Far East, and later, was under the command of the semi-retired, sixty-eight year old German Field Marshal Alfred Count von Waldersee, proposed by the Tsar of Russia.

On May 28, 1900, British ambassador, Claude Maxwell MacDonald, in the Legation Quarter in Beijing, feeling the threat, requested reinforcement. At the time, seventeen British warships were anchoring near Dagu port outside of Tianjin. Upon request, they dispatched 337 marines, who landed on May 31. Germany and Austria also send marines to join the Alliance Army. Five hundred men traveled to Beijing by train before the Boxers destroyed the railroad.

Dagu was a fortification outside of Tianjin. It was the first line of defense against invasion. However, after the Chinese defeat of the Second

Opium War in 1860, the treaty did not allow China to arm the Dagu fortification. Therefore, Tianjin was defenseless against any invasion from the sea. Enemy troops could land easily outside of Tianjin.

In Tianjin, the Boxers were attacking foreigners, Chinese Christians, and burning churches. They went to Viceroy's palace and requested Viceroy of Zhili, Yong Lu, for the ammunition. Yong Lu could not refuse. Soon, the Boxers ransacked his arsenal.

The Alliance reinforced their military presence significantly. On June 10, the Alliance took the Dagu Fort without much resistance. It paved the way for the landing of further Alliance troops. The landed Alliance troops started the siege on Tianjin. The capture of Tianjin was within days of reach.

In June, due to the destruction of railroad and telegraph lines by the Boxers, the communications between Tianjin and Beijing were broken down. It isolated Qing Army stationed in Tianjin.

The siege went on for one month. On July 9, General Nie of Huai Army died in a combat defending Tianjin. On July 14, Tianjin fell and the Deputy Viceroy of Zhili, Yu Lu committed suicide. The Muslim troops retreated to set up defense lines between Tianjin and Beijing.

When the Eight-Nation Alliance captured Tianjin, it took revenge by slaughtering Chinese. German, Russian and French army engaged in indiscriminate killing, raping, robbing civilians and burning the buildings. One third of the city was burned down. The Alliance troops eagerly raped women. The Germans and Russians behaved savagely. They bayoneted their rape victims. Disgusted American marines attempted to restrain the Germans with violence. The Alliance covered up their atrocities by labeling all Chinese they killed as Boxers, and Western reporters were one-sidedly biased.

Among the foreigners, besieging Tianjin was a young American mining engineer named Herbert Hoover, who would be a future President of the United States.

Expedition of Seymour

In mid June, while the siege of Tianjin was going on fervently, British commander Edward Seymour led an Alliance force of 2,000 Marines, the largest British contingent, to march from Dagu to Beijing. The troops rode the train from Dagu to Tianjin.

Figure 10 British Commander Seymour

However, the railway between Tianjin and Beijing had been severed. At first, Seymour resolved to repair the railroad. As Seymour later realized that the damage was beyond repair, on June 19, he abandoned the hope to go by train, and decided to march toward Beijing on foot along the railroad. From Tianjin to Beijing, it was only eighty miles. Seymour determined that without resistance, his troop could arrive in Beijing in three to four days.

When Seymour's Alliance troop moved toward Beijing, Qing Court issued a warning and ordered Seymour to stop. Prince Duan issued Court orders to Imperial Army to attack Seymour's troop immediately. Nevertheless, Rong Lu, who was the supreme commander of the Qing Army in the Province of Zhili, considered that the war was not formally declared and he still tried to negotiate a peace, withheld the order. The Chinese troops nearby did not take any action while the Alliance troop advanced.

On June 21, when Qing Court declared the war, Rong Lu released the order to attack. By then, the Alliance was already half way on the road to Beijing.

When the Alliance troop approached LangFang, a small town south of Beijing, they met with the Muslim troops led by General Ma Fu Xiang, stationed at Hunting Park. The Muslim troop launched the attack on the Alliance troop. The Chinese force included cavalry of 5,000 men, armed with modern magazine rifles. The Chinese feinted first with the Boxers masking the Muslim troops, when the Alliance troops attacked, the Boxers dispersed and the Muslim troops opened fire.

As the Alliance army was out-numbered, Seymour decided to retreat from LangFang, They moved southward toward the Peiho River. The Muslim troops pursued. Along the retreat, they met with stiff attacks and suffered over two hundred wounded by the time they reached the riverbank.

They took four civilian Chinese junks in the river, loaded the wounded soldiers as well as supplies onto the junks and pulled them along with ropes from the riverbanks. They were very low on food, ammunition and medical supplies. The Boxer and Qing Armies also surrounded them. The situation became critical. They decided to call the reinforcement, rather than risking the adventure alone.

They found a defensible position, and waited for rescue. They used Chinese informants to help them infiltrate through the Boxer and Qing lines, informing them of their predicament. Surrounded and attacked nearly around the clock by Qing troops and Boxers, their situation was desperate.

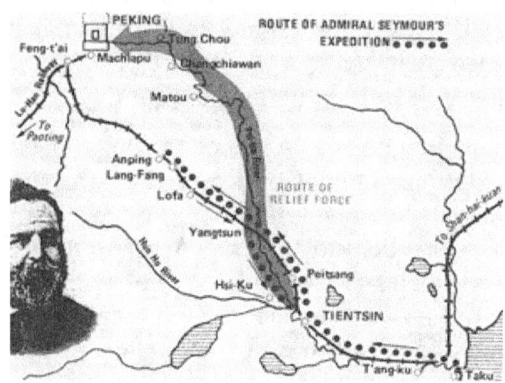

Figure 11 The Seymour expedition (dot), and Gaselee expedition (gross line)

On 25 June, a regiment composed of 1,800 men, with 900 Russian troops from Port Arthur, 500 British seamen, and mix of other Western nationalities arrived to reinforce Commander Seymour.

With the arrival of reinforcement, the Alliance troops lifted the siege and captured the Xigu Arsenal. Xigu Arsenal was a hidden Qing munitions' cache that the Western Powers had not previously known. In the Arsenal, they discovered not only German Krupp-made field guns, but also rifles with millions of rounds in ammunition, along with millions of pounds of rice and ample medical supplies. Taking the field guns and food supply, and setting fire to any munitions that they could not take, they departed from the Xigu Arsenal in the early morning of June 26.

The Seymour's expedition retreated to Tianjin by late June 26, and ended as a total failure for the Alliance.

The Qing Army successfully stopped the advance of Alliance troops for the time being. Dong Fu Xiang became a national hero in China. His troop also inflicted heavy casualties on Russian Army in Shanhaiguan, the fort at the Great Wall. The Muslim troop gained fame in the West.

The defeat of the Alliance Expedition met uproar in the West. People were crying for revenge. A wave of anti-Chinese sentiment arose in Europe.

Media in the West portrayed China as an evil empire and cried for vengeance. Ironically, the invaders felt that they were the violated.

Gaselee Expedition

Soon, the Alliance repositioned itself and organized another expedition. On July 14, the Alliance appointed the British Lieutenant-General Alfred Gaselee to lead a combined force. This time, the combined troop had 20,000 soldiers consisting of Russian, Japanese, British forces and assorted troops from other nationalities.

On August 4, 1900, General Alfred Gaselee's expedition left Tianjin. It defeated the Chinese army at Beicang on August 5. The Chinese army retreated approximately 12 miles to Yancun where it took up prepared positions between the east bank of the Hay River and a railroad embankment.

Yancun was the strong point at which the Chinese army hoped to stop the advance of the Alliance army. The country was flat, with little cover for the attackers, except for fields of millet and corn, and the 30-foot high railroad embankment gave shelter to the Chinese army.

The Americans and British were in one of the Alliance columns advancing on Yangcun on August 6. The Japanese remained on the west side of the Hay River. The Chinese troop numbered about 15,000 nearby. The weather was extremely hot and humid. It posted a serious problem for Alliance soldiers. Marching under the scorching sun without enough portable water, many men fell out of the ranks during the march, and some died by sunstroke. The heat incapacitated many others to fight the battle.

The attack began near noon, and what transpired was more of an endurance contest than a battle. Most of the men had already exhausted the water in their canteens. "There were neither wells nor streams of water in the country over which the advance was made. The men were famishing of thirst. They fell by scores with heat exhaustion.

The Muslim cavalry constantly fired upon them, and Chinese Muslim artillery bombarded their positions. The Alliance troop could not locate the Chinese artillery, which was raining shells upon their positions. The Chinese villages were nests for Imperial Chinese army and Boxer resistance, and

Chinese snipers poured fire out of loopholes, killing any foreigner who stepped out onto the streets. The snipers proved impossible to remove.

Chinese artillery had excellent accuracy, tearing straight through the Allied military barracks. The Eight-Nation Alliance troops were held in check by 15,000 Chinese braves. The artillery-caused casualties continually built up. A group of Alliance soldiers narrowly escaped after Chinese artillery shells almost destroyed their stronghold.

The Chinese artillery bombardment had finally exhausted the Alliance's patience, and they determined to put it to a halt. The Italians and British sought to sortie and to destroy the Chinese artillery. When the Italian attack commenced, they marched toward the Chinese troops, but were hit by heavy Chinese fire. They fled in terror and retreated. The Italian Lieutenant was severely wounded.

The Americans bore the brunt of the Chinese resistance as they advanced on the strongest Chinese positions behind the railroad embankment. The plain in front of them was like a furnace. Dust rose in thick clouds. Men collapsed of sunstroke and heat exhaustion. Chinese artillery and rifle fire was moderately severe and the Americans, now in an open country with no cover, advanced in a rush to dislodge the Chinese. However, as they charged over the embankment, they found most of the Chinese positions deserted. The remainder of the battle consisted of rear-guard actions as the Chinese covered their retreat.

As effective as the Muslim troops were, when the Alliance continued to reinforce to 45,000 men strong, they were hopelessly outnumbered. Yong Lu was hoping to achieve a truce with the Alliance. He was reluctant to call reinforcement from Huai Army in Shandong under Yuan Shi Kai. Unknown to the Alliance, Chinese troops received the orders not to continue to fight in order to facilitate the negotiation.

The Battle of Yangcun was over by late afternoon with the victorious but exhausted Alliance soldiers in control of the battlefield. The Chinese army had retreated with few casualties, abandoning strong positions as the Alliance soldiers advanced.

The Alliance had defeated the Chinese at both Beicang and Yangcun. After the fall of Yangcun, the defense line of the Muslim troops was no longer intact. The Alliance troops marching on different fronts could bypass some of the Muslim troops and advanced toward Beijing.

Although still intact and barely damaged, the Chinese army did not challenge the Alliance again about Yong Lu, and the Alliance soldiers continued their march, mostly unopposed, to Beijing. Yong Lu unilaterally gave up the defense in exchange of peaceful negotiation.

On August 14, the Alliance troop led by Commander Gaselee entered Beijing; relieved the Siege of the Legations, occupied the city and its surrounding countryside, and wiped out the last vestiges of the Boxer movement.

On another front, 1,200 miles northeast of Beijing in Manchuria, Russians took the advantage of the chaos in Zhili, opened another war zone trying to grab Manchuria. On July 16, 1900, Russian trooped occupied Hailanpao, a border town between China and Russia. Between July 16 and 21, Russian army killed 8,000 Chinese civilians.

Manchu Eight Banner Army defended the invasion. The banner men were annihilated as they fought to the death against the Russians, each falling one at a time against a five-pronged Russian invasion. When the Russian invasion started, while Chinese treated Russian civilians leniently and allowed them to escape to Russia, even notifying them since a state of war existed, that they should leave the war zone; by contrast, Russian Cossacks brutally killed Chinese civilians who tried to flee the villages.

The Chinese summoned all available men to fight, and the Chinese forces and garrisons gathered artillery and bombarded Russian troops and towns across the Amur River. Despite the Cossacks repulsing Chinese army crossings into Russia, the Chinese army troops increased the amount of artillery and kept up the bombardment.

In revenge for the attacks on Chinese villages, the Chinese troops burned Russian towns and almost annihilated a Russian force at Tieling. However, eventually Russians overpowered the Manchu troops, which were retreating and fleeing to the south. Along the way to pursue the retreating Banner men, Russians killed many soldiers and civilians alike. The Russian Cossacks looted their villages and property and then burnt them to ashes. Manchuria was completely occupied after the fierce fighting.

Siege of the Legation

Earlier in Beijing, on 31 May, over 3,000 diplomats, foreign civilians, soldiers, and Chinese Christians retreated to the Legation Quarter. The

Legation Quarter was a concession and settlement in Beijing for foreign embassies and residences after the signing of the Treaty for the Second Opium War in 1860. Most foreigners congregated in the Legation Quarter. Naturally, it became a target of the Boxers.

Before the siege had started, the foreign embassies in Beijing requested Alliance for reinforcement. The Alliance dispatched a troop of 500 navy men of different nationalities by train from Dagu to Beijing. At that time, both sides had not declared war yet, the Alliance soldiers could move by train without being stopped by the Qing Army. After they arrived in Beijing, these troops joined the Legations and set up their defense. The siege would last for fifty-five days.

The Legation in Beijing remained under siege from Boxer forces from June 20 to August 14. A total of 473 foreign civilians, plus the newly arrived soldiers, and about 3,000 Chinese Christians took refuge in the Legation Quarter under the command of the British Ambassador, Claude Maxwell McDonald. The staff and security personnel defended the compound with small arms, machine guns, and one old muzzle-loaded cannon.

Figure 12 A view of the Legation

On June 21, Qing Court declared war on Eight-Nation Alliance. By that time, Alliance already effectively encircled Tianjin. At the same time, more Alliance troops were advancing from Tianjin to Beijing. The large-scale assault from the Alliance was imminent, as soon as further reinforcement arrived.

On June 23, 1900, in Beijing, the Boxer rebels started setting fire to an area south of the British Legation, using it as a "frightening tactic" to attack the defenders. Hanlin Institute was a complex of courtyards and buildings that housed the oldest and richest library in the world, including the Yongle Encyclopedia.

The Yongle Encyclopedia was compiled in the early fifteenth century. It covered an array of subjects, including agriculture, art, astronomy, drama, geology, history, literature, medicine, natural sciences, religion and technology, as well as descriptions of unusual natural events. The encyclopedia, which was completed in 1408, comprised twenty three thousand manuscript rolls, or chapters, in eleven thousand volumes and using 3.7 billion Chinese characters.

The Hanlin Institute was nearby Sir Claude MacDonald, the commander-in-chief and he had become worried that the Boxer rebels might try to burn the Hanlin Institute. On June 24, 1900, when the winds shifted, the anticipated worry happened: Hanlin Institute's compound of buildings had caught fire, and the fire spread quickly. An attempt was made to save the Yongle Encyclopedia without success.

The Manchu authority blamed the British for setting the fire, whereas the British pointed to the direction of the wind, and claimed that it was either the Boxer rebels or the Manchu soldiers who set fire to the Hanlin. At the end of disaster, out of 11,000 volumes of the 400 hundred years old Yongle Encyclopedia, only fewer than four hundred volumes had been saved from the burning, causing irreparable loss to the world heritage.

The dove faction and hawk faction in the Qing Court continued to squabble against each other when the enemy troops were already approaching Beijing. The dove-faction Qing Princes offered the foreigners' shelters in the Zongli Yamen, and unilaterally declared a cease-fire from July 14 to August 4 and sent food and supplies to the Legation.

At the same time, Chinese troops captured the east French Legation, and unleashed a bombardment upon the French; the French position quickly turned into a death trap. On July 13, the Chinese mining explosives partially demolished the French legation.

The Chinese Imperial Army and Boxer snipers, aided with Chinese artillery, surrounded the partially demolished French Legation, maintaining a constant watch to prevent people from escaping. The casualty was mounting quickly inside of the Legation, soon reaching 200. The sniper casualties were indiscriminating, including French, British, American and Chinese alike.

Furthermore, under siege in Beijing was the North Cathedral, the Beitang, of the Catholic Church. There were 43 French and Italian soldiers, 33 Catholic Priests and nuns, and about 3,200 Chinese Catholics in the church. The defenders suffered heavy casualties, especially from lack of food and Chinese mines exploded in tunnels dug beneath the compound.

Conquest of Beijing

When Alliance marched toward Beijing, the Muslim troops were still in Beijing to defend the City. However, Rong Lu ordered them to withdraw in order to facilitate the negotiation. As the result, the Alliance troops entered the Capital without facing much resistance.

The Alliance occupied Beijing on August 14. All the nationalities in the international force raced to be the first to liberate the besieged Legation Quarter with the British winning the race. The U.S. played a minor role, in suppressing the Boxer Rebellion using her ships and troops deployed in the Philippines. In the U.S. military, the suppression of the Boxer Rebellion was known as the China Relief Expedition.

Figure 13 Alliance soldiers in the Forbidden City

The Occupation Beijing, Tianjin, and other cities in northern China lasted for more than one year by the Alliance force under the command of German General von Waldersee. The German force arrived too late to take part in the fighting, but undertook several punitive expeditions to the countryside against the Boxers. Although atrocities by foreign troops were common, German troops, in particular, were criticized for their barbaric behaviors.

The Germans were not the only offenders. French troops ravaged the countryside around Beijing. Nor were the soldiers of other nationalities behaved much better. The Russian soldiers were ravishing the women and committed horrible atrocities The Japanese was noted for their skill in beheading Boxers or people suspected of being Boxers.

The Alliance forces went on a killing, looting, and raping rampage against Chinese civilians on a massive scale. Many Chinese women and girls committed suicide to avoid being raped, including the fiancé of the future Regent Zai Feng.

In Beijing, Bishop Pierre-Marie-Alphonse Favier posted a bulletin: in the first eight days after August 18, Catholic Christians may steal life necessities, and declared that robbing needed no reporting. On December 14, 1900, a French newspaper quoted a soldier's statement: "We are open to the Church from the North palace, the priests go with us. They encourage us murder, robbery, robbing. We are doing for the priests. We were ordered to do whatever we want in the city for three days, kill if want to kill, take if want to take, and the actual looting of the eight days."

The Alliance troops also looted the Forbidden City. Countless of national treasure was lost. It mirrored the invasion in 1860, forty years ago.

Foreign media described the fighting going on in Beijing, as well as the alleged torture and murder of captured foreigners. Their reports were largely one-sided.

Exile to Xian

As late as July, CiXi was so confident about winning the battles, especially after the victory at the battle of LangFang. She again executed a few officers who dared to beg her for negotiation. In early August, she was utterly surprised that the Eight-Nation Alliance troop was approaching Beijing. By the time, the Eight-Nation Alliance troop marched toward Beijing; there were 50,000 soldiers strong. On August 14, the troop of Eight-Nation Alliance entered Beijing.

That night, CiXi, hearing the remote gunshots and explosions clearly from Forbidden City, could not sleep. Half of the sky was red as illuminated by fire.

CiXi could not help but sobbing. This was the second time the invading enemy was entering Beijing since 1644, the year that the last emperor of Ming Dynasty, ChongZhen committed suicide. The place that the last Ming Emperor ChongZhen died was only few miles away from where CiXi was.

Ironically, Beijing, Capital of the Ming Dynasty, fell into the hands of rebel force, organized by the peasants, not unlike the Boxers. Moreover, soon Manchu, itself the invading foreign power, not unlike the Eight-Nation Alliance, took control of Beijing and established a new dynasty. CiXi could not believe the event turned into such a disaster. She was wondering, "Was the history repeating?" CiXi regretted that she did not listen to those officers begging CiXi not to support the Boxers and declare the war. She felt so sorry for them that they died for her own good. Why she did not listen to them? CiXi also felt remorseful about herself. She started to hate herself and hate Prince Duan, who led her into such a miserable situation.

She remembered well the second time when enemy invaded Beijing. It was forty years ago and it was her personal experience. It was during the second Opium war. Britain and France jointly invaded China for opium trade. She was barely twenty-five years old. She had been a consort for Emperor XianFeng for eight years and bore a child for XianFeng, the future Emperor TongZhi. When they exiled from the Forbidden City, her son TongZhi was only four years old. Her husband, Emperor XianFeng, was already physically fragile, could not endure the hardship, died in the exile at the age of thirty-one. He left a vulnerable young CiXi and five-year-old son. The court was full of power hungry princes, who would not hesitate to crash her upon her return to the Forbidden City. Her life and her son's life were in grave danger.

Chapter 4

Yehenara Curse

It was 1852, when China was in the civil war of Taiping Rebellion. CiXi was barely eighteen years old. CiXi's family, Yehenara, belonged to one of the largest clans of Manchu. Yehenara clan was partly Mongol and partly Manchu. Yehenara had been a rival of the Qing royal clan, Aisin Giolo, for centuries before the founding of Qing Dynasty. Aisin Giolo clan, under the leadership of Nuerhachi, conquered most of Manchu tribes to unify Manchuria. In 1589, Nuerhachi married the daughter of Yehenara's chieftain. Her name was Meng Gu. His intention was to unite his strongest rival, Yehenara clan, by marriage.

However, shortly after Meng Gu's father, Yang Ji Nu, died, her brother, Nalin Bulu, inherited the chieftain position, and he was not content to subordinate under Nuerhachi. Soon, dispute escalated into war. Meng Gu, caught in between and saddened by the dispute between her husband and her brother, fell ill. She wanted to see her mother. When Nuerhachi requested to Meng Gu's brother, Nalin Bulu, to bring her mother, Nalin Bulu refused. Soon, Meng Gu died at the age of twenty-nine, without being able to see her mother for the last time. Nuerhachi vented the anger on Nalin Bulu. A war was erupted between two clans.

When one of Nuerhachi generals captured Nalin Bulu, he killed himself, before Nuerhachi could stop him. He cursed before he died, "We, Yehenara, swear to destroy you. Even we have only one woman left." The curse was imprinted in Aisin Gioro's minds. CiXi eventually fulfilled the curse not by conquering from outside, but by corrupting it from within.

At the age of fifty-seven, in 1616, Nuerhachi proclaimed himself as the Emperor of Da Jin. In 1625, he had defeated the Viceroy of Liaodong of the Ming Dynasty, by capturing the last stronghold of Ming Dynasty in Manchuria, and established Da Jin's capital in Shenyang, later also known as Mukden. In 1626, while Nuerhachi launched another campaign against Ming, he died on the road. His son, Huang Tai Ji, changed the name Da Jin into Qing. Huang Tai Ji therefore became the first emperor of Qing Dynasty – Emperor TaiZong.

It was not until 1644, when Huang Tai Ji's son, Emperor ShunZhi, entered the Great Wall, captured Beijing, and replaced the Ming Dynasty to become the official ruler of China.

Laner

According to Qing's royal custom, when the emperors became adult, the Court would select candidates for concubines and consorts among the eight largest Manchu clans. Yehenara was one of the clans. Although for many generations, Yehenara clan had been excluded from the selection, because of the curse, by the mid of the nineteenth century, the curse had been over two hundred years, and long forgotten. No one paid more attention to the ancient curse.

CiXi, who had a maiden name of Laner, grew up in Anhui, the birth-place of Huai Army. Her father, Huizheng, was a minor local officer. Laner had a younger sister, Rong Er, and a brother, Guei Xiang. Later, Rong Er married Emperor XianFeng's brother, Prince Chunqing. They produced the future Emperor GuangXu. Guei Xiang's daughter became Empress GuangXu's wife – Empress LongYu.

Her family was not poor, but their lifestyle was far from the extravaganza of the royal family. Her father's career went up and down. When Laner was fourteen years old, her father lost his job. Without suitable connections, he could not get another appointment. Years of unemployment drained most of the family savings.

Laner was beautiful, intelligent and talented. She was proficient in both Manchu and Chinese languages. She studied hard and was a quick learner. She was also skillful in calligraphy, painting and the art of arranging flowers.

She had a good voice and she liked to sing. Her father taught her to sing folk songs and operas. Father and daughter often sang together to entertain themselves. Since then, Laner was in love with operas. Before her father lost the job, she liked to watch operas in the theater. Later, when she became Empress Dowager, watching opera was one of her favorite pastimes.

When Laner was at the age of puberty, she could not even afford to dress up. Her father, loving her very much, always felt sorry for her. When she was seventeen, Huizheng caught lung disease, and fell ill. The family could ill afford doctors. The family pawned every valuable they had and could not save father's life. The family even had to beg for donation from their friends for the funeral expense.

Laner's mother, Tongjia, decided to move back to Beijing, their hometown, carrying father's coffin. They used the remaining money, charted a boat to travel by the Grand Canal. It took days to arrive in Beijing. Tongjia remembered a long time ago, when Huizheng took the job in Anhui, they traveled the same route from Beijing. How happy they were at that time.

They still maintained a home in Beijing. After leaving vacant for many years, it desperately needed repair. Laner's mother buried the husband, cleaned the house, and settled down. The old memory came back to her.

Laner was born in this house. She still had childhood playmates, her neighbors whom she had not seen for years. They were happy to see her back. With neighbors' help, Laner's mother worked on some odd, cleaning jobs, making some petty money to get by. Soon, the Spring came.

One day, Laner came home in a hurry. For several days, she did not venture out. Mother was curious and asked, "What happened? Why don't you go out to look for your friends?"

Laner said, "You know the eunuchs were visiting Manchu families. When they see young girls, they will draft them to serve in the palace."

Laner's mother thought that it was not a bad idea. At least, Laner could get a job and make some money. She told Laner so. Laner started to cry, "I don't want to go to the palace." Her mother did not insist.

However, the "destiny" would not be the "destiny" if one could escape from it. Few days later, the Palace envoy knocked on the door, "Is this family of Yehenara?"

When Laner's mother answered the door, the envoy asked to see her daughters. It was not an edict neither Laner's mother could refuse, nor did she want to. When Laner appeared, her beauty overwhelmed the envoy. Her name immediately went to the top of the list.

After the envoy left, Laner had cried for a few days. Only with mother's consolation, she came to accept it. "Who knows that it is the way out of family's destitute situation?" She reminded herself.

After detail investigation of her family background, Laner had met all the qualifications of the candidate of a concubine: She was a Manchu, was beautiful, and was younger than twenty years. Her father and grandfather had served in the government as middle level officers.

Few days later, when Laner received the notice of enlistment, together with a set of beautiful attire, she started to feel different. When she tried the attire, she felt the warmth in her heart at least temporarily. The expensive silk, the workmanship, the design of the attire all had a rich man's touch. Laner had the first taste of being rich.

Three days later, the carriage from the palace arrived. It was the first time that Laner was leaving the family. Mother and daughter cried together. Mother said, "Go ahead. It is not the end of the world. You will have a good time in the palace. Just don't forget us." Laner promised.

Tongjia, Guei Xiang, and Rong Er saw her off as far as they could go. This fateful moment changed the history of China forever. Laner was on her way to become the absolute ruler of China for forty-eight years to come. In addition, she did not forget her promise. Later she would make her brother Guei Xiang a high officer in the Qing Court and her sister to marry a prince. She would make both her sister's son and her brother's grandson emperors of China.

Consort Lan

When Laner entered the Forbidden City for the first time, she was awed and charmed. She could never imagine people lived in such grand and magnificent buildings. The doors were huge guarded by large bronze lions and the courtyard was wide and infinite. Yellow and blue roofs, supported by the colorful brackets, shined on the reflecting sunshine. Red wooden columns embraced by carved clawed dragons. Intricately carved figures decorated doors and window frames. It seemed like a dream to Laner, "Am I going to live here?"

However, she did not stay long in the Forbidden City. After doing some paper work, a carriage again took her outside of Beijing. She later learned that it was the Yuanming Garden, located at the northwestern outskirt of Beijing.

Together with Laner, there were sixty-four selected candidates in total for the concubines. Each one was assigned a quarter in the Yuanming Garden, waiting for the Emperor to visit, who would decide the fate of the candidate. There was no telling how long it would take.

Slowly, Laner adjusted to her new environment. It was not large but comfortable. It had a garden for its own. The backside of the quarter was by the lake. She had a nice and ample view to the other side of the lake in the distance. The surrounding was shadowed by the pine-oak mixed broad-leaved deciduous forests. It smelt refreshing unlike her home always musty. In front the quarter, a path led to a main road. Later, Laner learned that this was one of the main roads connecting the Garden entrance to Emperor Residence in the Garden.

Days went by in the Royal Garden. Initially, Laner was excited. She cleaned up her quarter, practiced her calligraphy and her painting, read books. After several weeks, she felt isolated and boring. She started to miss home.

She received a monthly stipend, which was not much, but better than she could make by working outside. She kept some money for herself and sent the rest home to her mother. She also realized that she relied on her maids and eunuchs for many of the things she wanted to do, for example, to send letters to and receive letters from her home. With her saved money, she could tip the maids and eunuchs handsomely. Very soon, they were eager to serve her.

Laner learned that Emperor came and went quite often from Yuanming Garden to the Forbidden City. Normally, he did not take the route passing Laner's quarter. Laner devised a plan, and bribed the eunuchs to detour Emperor's route to pass in front of her quarter.

Not much later, her servants told her that the Emperor would come to her way. She immediately prepared herself, put on her best dress, and waited. When she heard the Emperor's entourage coming, she started to sing. Her vibrating voice filled the air. When Emperor heard the singing, he asked, "Who sings this beautifully?"

The eunuch answered, "She is one of the candidates for the concubine whom we recently enlisted."

Emperor requested to stop the entourage and wanted to see her. When Emperor entered the front yard of Laner's quarter, Laner pretended that she did not notice, continued to sing inside the quarter. Her voice enchanted the Emperor. He did not disturb until Laner had finished her singing. Emperor clapped hands and applauded. Laner acted as if suddenly she felt the presence of Emperor, let out a gasp of surprise, and kneeled down to greet the Emperor and asked for forgiveness.

When the Emperor saw Laner, Laner's beauty immediately attracted him. Her young face was radiant with the air of innocence and wit. He spent the afternoon with Laner. The second day, Emperor sent eunuchs to fetch her. Eunuchs called her "Lady Lan." She knew that the Emperor conferred her title. She became an official concubine. Laner had achieved her first goal.

Emperor XianFeng was only four years older than Laner was. He was twenty-two years at the time. He was married to Empress XiaoZhen, of the same age. They had no child. Empress XiaoZhen was an uncunning and unsophisticated person, a typical homemaker. She was no match for Laner's wit, now the Lady Lan. Lady Lan befriended XiaoZhen. Although Empress XiaoZhen would sometimes be jealous of Lady Lan, but there was no shortage of women for XiaoZhen as she realized. Lady Lan was not the only one. In addition, Lady Lan's amicable attitude to her and treating her with respect won her heart. These two women would be together for long time to come. For the reason of the location of the palaces, they resided. Later, Lady Laner would be known as the West Empress Dowager and XiaoZhen would be known as the East Empress Dowager.

In the third year that Lady Lan met Emperor XianFeng, she was pregnant. Emperor was overjoyed. When the child was born, it was a boy – the first boy of Emperor XianFeng, an heir apparent to the throne. It was a major celebration event for the country. Lady Lan was promoted as Consort Lan, and the newborn son was christened as Zai Chun, the future Emperor TongZhi. Consort Zhen further consolidated her position in the Qing Court.

Emperor XianFeng had a brother, Price Chunqing. When Consort Lan heard that Price Chunqing's wife recently deceased, she proposed to Emperor XianFeng to let Prince Chunqing to marry her sister Rong Er. Prince Chunqing and Rong Er later produced a son, who would be the future Emperor GuangXu. Consort Lan had a niece, Rong Lu, who was much more capable than her brother was. She also arranged a position in the military for him. Rong Lu, expressed his gratitude, and later, would serve Consort Lan in the most critical conditions for his life.

When Lady Laner was with Emperor XianFeng, she would advise XianFeng not to ignore the reports and memorials submitted by the court officers, because they were the daily matter of the nation. Since Lady Lan wrote well, soon XianFeng used her as secretary. He would dictate his comments and decisions to Lady Laner to write on the memorials. Gradually, he even asked Lady Laner to review the memorials for him. Over the time, Lady Laner became familiar with the subject of matter and started to make decisions on behave of Emperor XianFeng.

In Qing Court tradition, women were not allowed to interfere with the policy-making. It was an unspoken institutional practice to prevent women from holding power. What Consort Lan did clearly was exploring the taboo of conduct as perceived by some court officers. These officers were uneasy by Consort Lan's interference in the policy-making and strongly advised Emperor XianFeng not to let this continue. Consort Lan had made influential enemies in the court. Among them, Sushun was the most powerful one.

Sushun was probably the most capable Manchu court official in the nineteenth century. If without CiXi, he would take control of the power after Emperor XianFeng died in 1862. China would be a very different country.

Sushun belonged to the Aisin Gioro clan, the bloodline of Manchu royal family; the direct descendent of Aisin Gioro Jierhalang, Nuerhachi's niece and adopted son and one of the founding fathers of Qing Dynasty. Jierhalang was also the co-regent of Emperor ShunZhi, who effectively was the first Qing Emperor to rule the entire China.

Sushun served as the head of royal cabinet under Emperor XianFeng. He was fifteen years senior of XianFeng. He was farsighted, decisive, capable of using talented people, whether Manchu or Han equally. It was his decision to use Han officers like Zeng Guo Fan to organize Xiang Army to defeat the Taiping Rebellion and Zuo Zong Tang to put down the Muslim Rebellion in western China. He served Emperor XianFeng's father – Emperor DaoGuang. He was the most powerful man in the Qing Court besides Emperor. He had not seen Consort Lan as a threat but only as a minor disturbance and irritation, because the balance of power was heavily tilted toward him. His oversight eventually costed his life.

Sushun's open criticism to Consort Lan in front of Emperor XianFeng alarmed Consort Lan. She knew then that without getting rid of Sushun, eventually it would spell the end of her life. She was determined to find a way to crush her enemy. However, she was not in the power to do so yet.

While the war against the Taiping Rebellion was still raging on, another trouble with the international powers was brewing.

Second Opium War

Harry Smith Parkes was a junior diplomat in 1840's. He had studied Chinese in Macao. During the first Opium war, he served as secretary and translator to the British representative, later, the first Governor of Hong Kong, Henry Pottinger. In 1854, he became the British Consul in Xiamen. Not much later, he was transferred to Guangzhou.

On October 8 1856, a Chinese cargo ship sailing from Xiamen to Guangzhou was unloading at the Guangzhou port. The soldiers went aboard to search upon receiving a tip that the ship carried smuggled merchandize. Several people were apprehended and the smuggled merchandize was confiscated. The owner of the ship as well as the crews was Chinese. Nevertheless, the ship was registered in Hong Kong. At that time, it was a common practice to register ships in Hong Kong in order to avoid the inspection by the Chinese Custom. However, the owner of the ship reported the incident to the Hong Kong authority.

Parkes immediately seized the opportunity to demand the release of detained people and the return of the confiscated merchandize. Parkes claimed that the soldiers torn down the British flag, therefore, insulted the Britain. The Viceroy of Guangzhou, Ye Ming Chen, thought it was a minor incident, released the detained people the next day. However, Parkes would not buckle, and asked the Viceroy to apologize personally to him. Viceroy Ye ignored the request. On October 23, British warships attacked Guangzhou. Qing Court tried to negotiate, but could not accept the British demand. While Emperor XianFeng was indecisive, Britain dispatched more warships anchoring outside of Tianjin.

Meanwhile, another excursion with France facilitated the alliance of Britain and France. A French Catholic Father ventured into Guangxi Province without permission. In a dispute with local people, he was killed. The incident resulted in French protest.

The Last Days of An Empire

In December 1857, the joint British French troop of six thousand soldiers invaded Gaugnzhou again. This time the invasion met with fierce resistance. Guangzhou fell to British and French army. British troop captured Viceroy Ye and sent him to India under house arrest. A year later, Ye died in protest by fasting.

After Guangzhou's fall, Britain and French gathered warships sailing north to anchor outside of Dagu near Tianjin port, and made further demand. Russia and the United States volunteered to be mediators. On one hand, Qing Court was preparing for the war; on the other hand, it was pinning hope on Russia and U.S. mediation.

However, British and France did not intend to stop the invasion. On May 20, on the pretention that mediation had failed, the British and French Alliance troop attacked Dagu. Soon, Dagu fell, and the Alliance troop entered Tianjin on May 26, and threatened to attack Beijing. Qing Court was in disarray, and sent a negotiation delegate to Tianjin. Britain and France signed the Tianjin Treaty, respectively with Qing Court on June 26, and 27. The treaty opened additional ten ports as free trades zones, including the ports on the upstream of Yangtze River, such as Hankou, six hundred miles from the coast. All foreign ships had the right to navigate freely in the Yangtze River. Missionaries were all free to preach inland of China. Foreigners were free to travel anywhere in China. China would also to pay Britain four million taels of silver and to pay France two million taels of silver as indemnity. As mediators, Russia and U.S. also obtained the same concessions from China except the indemnity. In addition, Russia made Qing Court to agree that the Chinese Russian borderline was still undefined, that it would be settled later. It paved the way for further Russian aggression to claim the Chinese territory in the future.

In November 1858, at the threat of Britain and France, the treaty was amended: Britain and France would take control of Chinese Custom in the treaty ports. They would impose 5% of export tax on all Chinese exports, and all the import tax would be limited to 2.5%. Of course, all the tax went to Britain and France.

British and France insisted on signing the amendment in Beijing, but Qing Court, which was afraid of disturbance in Beijing, preferred to sign in Shanghai. Nevertheless, under the insistence of the Britain and France, Qing Court conceded but only under the condition that the delegates should not be accompanied by military force, which Britain and France did not agree.

On June 25, 1859, Britain and France again attacked Dagu. Qing Court had previously reinforced the fortification, and appointed the Mongolian General Senggelinqin as commander, who successfully defeated the British and French attack.

When the news of British and French defeat reached Europe, it caused an outcry. The hawks in both countries were demanding revenge. In February 1860, both countries again sent troops totaling 21,000 soldiers to China.

In April 1860, the Alliance occupied Zhoushan, a port south of Shanghai. In May, it occupied Dalian in Manchuria and Yantai in Shandong.

After a small victory in Dagu, Qing Court thought it could defend itself. This time, General Senggelinqin committed a fatal error. He put all the defense force in Dagu, and ignored the other coast. When the Russian passed the intelligence that Beitang port at the north of Dagu was defenseless, the Alliance force detoured to the north. They landed without any resistance.

Once Alliance force avoided Dagu and landed in Beitang on August 1, it took the roundabout route and attacked Dagu on both sides, Dagu fortification fell on August 24.

Again, Qing Court sent envoy for negotiation, but could not accept the demand. The Mongol General Senggelinqin hated Parke. While in negotiation table, a dispute burst out, Senggelinqin ordered guards to round up Parke and detained him. British ambassador demanded the immediate release of Parke. Qing Court did not release Parke until the Alliance invaded Beijing.

On September 21, the battle erupted at Baliqiao, the last bastion between Tianjia and Beijing. After few days of fierce battle, again Baliqiao fell.

Russian spies took advantages of the newly granted freedom of travel for the foreigners to collect information of Chinese defense strategy. It passed the intelligence to the Alliance troop in exchange of other favors. The Alliance knew exactly the movement of Chinese defense troops, and set their strategy accordingly.

On October 13, the Alliance entered Beijing. It started massacre and looting. After Parke's release, he was so angry that he ordered the burning of Yuanming Garden as revenge.

On October 7, 1860, when British French Alliance troop entered Yuanming Garden, the looters took whatever they could manage to take, but destroyed those they could not take, causing irreplaceable loss to the treasure of the world. Some of the treasures were presented to the Queen of England and Napoleon III.

The same tragedy would repeat exactly forty years later. CiXi, as Consort Lan in 1860, was young and not responsible for the event. However, in 1900, she was old and largely responsible for what happened.

Exile to Jehol

While the British and French Alliance troop was marching toward Beijing, Emperor XianFeng was ill. XianFeng was frail and in bad physical condition. The invasion further added the mischief. Both XiaoZeng and Lan were serving at the bedside. One day late afternoon, Sushun and another court officer Duanhua were outside XianFeng's quarter to ask for an audience. Emperor XianFeng had the feeling that that the situation turned worse.

When they entered, Sushun reported the battle status, and commented: "We don't know how long we can hold on the defense. Enemies can attack Beijing in a day or two. I want to advise Your Highness to prepare for the retreat."

Emperor XianFeng hesitated, "Now it is getting dark, and I am sick, where can I go?"

After much discussion, Empress XiaoZhen suggested to go to Jehol. Jehol is outside of the Great Wall, at the border between Manchuria and Inner Mongolia. It is about 100 miles northeast of Beijing. Qing Court maintained a large Summer Palace there. Since the decision was made, Sushun advised that Emperor XianFeng to depart immediately. Reluctantly, XianFeng agreed. XianFeng asked his brother Prince Gong to stay behind and defend Beijing, Sushun to escort XianFeng and Duanhua to take care of the Yuanming Garden. In a moment of notice, Yuanming Garden went into action. There were only three carriages, two for the Emperor, Empress and the heir apparent, and other concubines, including Consort Lan. Others would have to walk. They were more like refugees rather than a royal cortege. Few days later, they arrived in the Summer Palace.

XianFeng was already very sick before he took the trip. The exile trip, without decent rests and meals, took heavy toll on his body. By the time he arrived in the Summer Palace, he was exhausted. When Prince Gong brought the demands from Britain and France, besides all the concessions on the sovereign rights, Britain wanted twelve million taels of silver and France wanted six million, XianFeng almost collapsed.

Sushun and Duanhua, who were rivals of Prince Gong, complained, "How can you report such notice to Emperor at this moment?"

XianFeng could not decide what to do with the demand, and consulted XiaoZhen and Lan. Xiao could not comment, but Lan vented, "Now that the enemies are in Beijing. We lost the war. If we do not agree, is there anything else we can do? We can only blame who could not defend. I say that the priority today is to make peace. The Taiping Rebellion and Nian Rebellion are still going on right now. We cannot afford to fight with foreigners anymore. Even if we want, surely we will lose again. Once we go back to Beijing, we will have time to think about what to do next." Prince Gong was grateful that Consort Lan saved the day for him.

This was exactly what XianFeng wanted – peace. He agreed to the terms of the treaty. Finally, after two years, the trouble with foreigners was over. It was the time to prepare to return Beijing.

Figure 14 Jehol Summer Palace

Nevertheless, Xian-Feng's health deteriorated day by day. He could not even focus to read the official reports anymore. He delegated the duty to Empress XiaoZhen. However, XiaoZhen did not understand much of the administration affair. She again asked Consort to review for XianFeng. Effectively, Consort Lan was managing the daily issues of the nation behind the curtain.

Sushun observed Consort Lan's motivation and movement clearly. He also realized that XianFeng's disease became terminal. Sometimes XianFeng retched with bloodstains in his handkerchief. Sushun would have to come up with a plan quickly to deal with Consort Lan after XianFeng died. He secretly called meetings with his diehard followers – Prince Zhengqing Duanhua, Staff of Grand Council Mu Yin, Prince Yiqing Zai Yuan, and several others to discuss a plot. He suggested deposing Consort Lan's heir apparent, or even better, killing the mother and the son, and electing Prince Yiqing as the emperor. Zai Yuan was not so audacious. He would like to be a regent only to help the young Emperor. Before they could find a workable plan, news arrived: "Emperor XianFeng died."

Consort Lan's Coup

Consort Lan was one-step ahead of Sushun. She hided the Imperial Jade Seal soon after XianFeng died. She used the Imperial Seal, wrote an edict in XianFeng's name, and ordered Prince Chunqing, Prince Gong, and Yong Lu to execute the plot that they had previously discussed.

When Sushun went to Empress XiaoZhen for the Seal, she told him that Prince Gong took it to Beijing. Sushun believed it. Empress XiaoZhen also implored Sushun to escort her with late Emperor's casket to Beijing. She did this on Consort Lan's request to slow down Sushun. Sushun's plan was to arrive in the Forbidden City one-step ahead of Consort Lan and used the seal to forge the edict to crown Prince Yiqing, then order the arrest of Consort Lan and her son, the heir apparent for treason. However, he underestimated Consort Lan.

By the time Sushun and Empress XiaoZhen departed, Yong Lu already was in Consort Lan quarter with another trusted aide. They soon fetched Consort Lan and Zai Chun, the heir apparent, rode on the horsebacks. They took the short cut and traveled fast and nonstop, and arrived in Beijing within one day, well ahead of Sushun, who was traveling with carriages.

When Consort Lan arrived in Beijing, the news of XianFeng's death barely arrived in Beijing. Immediately, she called an emergency audience of court officers in the name of last edict of XianFeng, to announce Zai Chun to ascent the throne, and changed the name of Chinese calendar year to TongZhi.

Rong Lu ordered his troops to apprehend Sushun's allies immediately after the audience. Sushun's allies were leaderless and were not aware of the change of situation when they were arrested. At the same time, Rong Lu led a squadron to meet Sushun half way to Jehol. Sushun was spending the night at Miyun, a small town twenty miles from Beijing, not expecting Rong Lu's arrival at midnight, caught in surprise, was arrested without putting a fight.

By a simple stroke, Consort Lan launched a coup to defeat a formidable enemy, and started her forty-eight years of ruling as China's supreme ruler. She was young then, however, she was merciless. Shortly, she executed Sushun and his diehard followers. She did this for preventing Sushun from coming back, and for demonstrating her authority. Since then, she held absolute power over the Qing Court. She changed her title to Empress Dowager CiXi, and officially became the Regent. That year, CiXi was only twenty seven year old.

Exile to Xian

These were the wee hours of August 15, 1900, CiXi stayed awake in her quarter the whole night. The past flashed through her mind like lucid and vivid pictures. The distant, muffled sound of gunfire came occasionally to wake her up from her immersion in the past. The sound of gunfire was not unlike the fireworks in the New Year. CiXi wondered if she could pass unscathed this time. She had spent so much money to build a new garden - Yihe Garden. Would the foreigners spare her garden this time?

She was trying to do the best for the country. She did not understand why her effort did not make the country better. War after the war, defeat after the defeat, treaty after the treaty, revolt after the revolt, they came with increasing frequency. She wondered what it would take to put a stop on all these. GuangXu was inexperienced. Capable officers were few. Corruption was rampant. New threats from revolutionaries were getting stronger. In addition, most difficult of all, she was getting older. She was sixty-five years old. She did not have the energy as used to have. How long she could hold onto this. After she died, what would happen to Qing? She thought she was smart and powerful, nevertheless, she could not find a solution to all these problems.

Her parents were long gone. She missed her father and mother. She remembered the day she left home to the palace. She faced an unknown future, for better or for worse. There had been no return. If her father had not died, they would have stayed in Anhui, and then she would not have gone to the palace. What would she be then? She would have married someone else, some ordinary people and lived an ordinary life. What difference it could make? Soon the day would break; it would be another day. What a terrible day!

On August 15, 1900, at dawn, while she was still engrossed in regret and sorrow, Prince Duan came running and flustered, crying, "Empress, foreign troops are approaching the gates of Forbidden City now! Your Highness needs to go." The nightmare came.

Li Lian Ying's voice urged, "Your Highness, we need to move soon."

CiXi woke up to the reality. She noticed that the sound of gunfire was intensifying and approaching. She immediately ordered the eunuchs start to pack, and sent Li to fetch the Emperor from Yantai and Consort Zhen from her quarter.

Death of Consort Zhen

In 1888, Empress CiXi selected her niece, Yehenara Jingfen, also GuangXu's cousin, as GuangXu's wife. Jingfen, two years senior of GuangXu, became Empress LongYu. They were closely related by blood: Jingfen's father was Guei Xian. GuangXu's mother was Rong Er, and CiXi was the Laner. They were brother and sisters. However, GuangXu disliked Jingfen from very early time, when they were playmates as kids, long before they were married. She was vulgar, inconsiderate, and not attractive. Few months after he was married, GuangXu selected the Tatara sisters to be his consorts, Zhen and her sister Jin. GuangXu fell in love with Consort Zhen at first sight. Consort Zhen, or Lady Tatara, was only thirteen years old. Consort Zhen was beautiful, smart, and confident. She was five years younger than GuangXu. Since then, GuangXu spent most of his time with his favorite consort, the Imperial Consort Zhen. She gave him encouragement, vision, and tenderness. It was the best time in his life.

At the beginning, CiXi did not have anything against Consort Zhen. However, out of jealousy, the out of favor Empress LongYu, always went to CiXi to complain and gossip about Consort Zhen. Gradually, CiXi became biased.

Before the Jiawu Sino-Japanese War, CiXi was inclined to negotiate, while GuangXu wanted to fight the war. Each one had supporters. Both sides were in deadlock. Consort Zhen's brother and royal teacher also sided with GuangXu. Sometimes, Consort Zhen was quite outspoken. CiXi felt that Consort Zhen behaved out of her place. CiXi developed dislike for

Consort Zhen. In addition, GuangXu always confided court matters with her. This made CiXi even more resentful. CiXi suspected that Consort Zhen influenced GuangXu heavily on the reform. It was ironic that CiXi started to get involved in Emperor XianFeng's business from early one, but she did not approve Consort Zhen to do the same.

That fateful morning, when GuangXu and Consort Zhen showed up, Consort Zhen asked CiXi to allow GuangXu stay. This was the first time since the end of "Hundred Days Reform" that GuangXu saw Consort Zhen. She was also under house arrest in a different place from GuangXu. It had been almost two years, since they had seen each other. How GuangXu was missing Consort Zhen. He could not imagine that he would see Consort Zhen again under this kind of circumstance. GuangXu felt that Consort Zhen was thinner and wasted away. She must have suffered in these two years. GuangXu had a strong urge to hold her, to spend time alone with her. GuangXu was glad that finally he could be with her again, despite the situation. However, he would not imagine what would happen next. It was also the last time he was seeing Consort Zhen.

Previously, CiXi had already been unhappy about the letter from foreigners that Prince Duan showed her. The letter, which was forged by Prince Duan, demanded GuangXu's release from house arrest. Prince Duan's letter, although forged, had the credibility to CiXi because it was consistent with the other happenings. Beforehand, British and French ambassadors had offered to send foreign doctors to treat GuangXu. They also warned not to depose GuangXu. CiXi was already jealous and felt threatened.

Now Consort Zhen's request was like a sword hitting her heart. She was most afraid that the foreigners would seize GuangXu depose her and used him as puppet emperor. Immediately, CiXi denied the request.

However, Consort Zhen did not know how to stop; she started to blame CiXi for what happened. CiXi became furious. The thunder-like gunfire was approaching. The invading foreign troops could arrive in any moment. It was putting pressure on her. Everybody was anxious to leave. The eunuchs were urging CiXi to move. CiXi suddenly was enraged. She vented the anger on Consort Zhen, "How dare you criticize me?"

Figure 15 GuangXu and Consort Zhen

Before GuangXu can stop Consort Zhen, Li Lian Ying ordered the servants to grab and hold down Consort Zhen, "How audacious you are! Kneel down and ask for forgiveness."

Consort Zhen became hysteric, struggled against the men holding her. Two years of house arrest was too much stressful for her. Now she had a chance to vent, she was crying that she refused to leave. She was hysterical. CiXi laughed coldly: "If you want to stay, you stay!"

She frostily ordered the eunuchs to push Consort Zhen into a nearby well. GuangXu was shocked beyond believe. He kneeled down in front of CiXi begging for mercy. However, CiXi had already lost her sense. She was mad. Despite GuangXu's imploring and crying she let the eunuchs to carry out her order. When GuangXu rushed over to save Consort Zhen, eunuchs pulled him back.

Consort Zhen struggled, crying, "Let me go!"

However, she was overpowered. When a thud followed by a short cry from the bottom of deep well, GuangXu suddenly lost his mind. He lost the only one who cared for him, the only one who understood him, and he could have the heart-to-heart talk. Consort Zhen was the only pleasure he had in his life. As long as there was Consort Zhen, GuangXu still had some hope. Without Consort Zhen, his life was meaningless. CiXi took controlled his life, since he was a child. Now she took away the most precious thing he had -his love. In addition, Consort Zhen was only twenty-four years old. GuangXu collapsed.

Only when Consort Zhen died, CiXi returned to reality. She realized that she had done, but it was too late. The gunfire was too close to be comfortable. At the urge of Li Lian Ying, she ordered the eunuchs to cover the well and moved.

When CiXi returned Beijing one year later, the first thing she did was to confer the honorable Imperial Consort title to Consort Zhen.

CiXi was debating where to go for exile. Jehol summer palace was too close to be safe. It was only one hundred miles from Beijing. Its location, half way between Beijing and Manchuria, made it a less desirable choice, because Russian Army was in Manchuria. Anywhere nearby the coast, such as Nanjing, was immediately ruled out because it was too vulnerable. The cities further upstream of Yangtze River, such as Wuhan or Chongqing, were not good choice either because the anti-Manchu sentiment was high there. Finally, CiXi selected Xian. It was remote, more than one thousand miles from the coast. Best of all, it was close to Gansu, the stronghold of the Muslim Army. In the worst case, CiXi could count on the protection of the Muslim Army and retreated to Gansu.

By August 17, CiXi's entourage, escorted by the Palace Security Guard dispatched by Yong Lu, arrived in Huailai County, about eighty miles northwest of Beijing, just south of the Great Wall. The County Magistrate Wu Yong Di came to welcome CiXi. CiXi finally had a good rest after two days of travel. The second day, when CiXi's entourage departed, Magistrate Wu dispatched more security guards to escort CiXi.

By August 21, they arrived in Xuanhua City, where they stayed for four days. CiXi issued an edict to ask the Viceroy of Shanxi Duan Fang to prepare their arrival in Xian. From Xuanhua, CiXi's entourage turned southwest, continued through Datong and arrived in Taiyuan on September 6.

Earlier in June, CiXi already transferred Li Hong Zhang to Zhili to negotiate with the Eight-Nation Alliance. Now the invasion was over, Li sent telegram to CiXi: "Your Majesty can safely return to Beijing now."

However, CiXi did not feel comfortable before Li concluded his negotiation. She continued to move on to Xian. As CiXi had expected, the Eight-Nation Alliance did not stop the invasion at the capture of Beijing. Instead, it increased its force to 100,000 soldiers and push inland. When Li Hong Zhang negotiated a deal with the Eight-Nation Alliance on September 7, 1901, the invasion troop already pushed into Shanxi Province, which is 300 miles inland of Tianjin.

Li's Negotiation

While the war was going on, Li Hong Zhang, under CiXi's instruction, contacted the Eight-Nation Alliance for a truce. The Eight-Nation Alliance put pressure on him. They asked him to stop the rampage before they would be willing to negotiate. Li Hong Zhang went to see Yong Lu, and told him about foreigners' demand.

Yong Lu contemplated and said, "From my point of view, even though the Muslim Army won an upper hand for the time being, but sooner or later, they would be out run. The less damage we inflicted on the foreigners, the less painful will be the negotiation."

Li Hong Zhang agreed. He asked Rong Lu to help, since Rong Lu was Dong Fu Xiang's superior. Only with Yong Lu's interfere, Dong Fu Xiang pulled back the attack on the Legations. The Legations avoided the total destruction. Dong also retreated in several fronts of his defense, notably at Yangcun, to comply Li's request. After the retreat from Yangcun, Yong Lu ordered his Army not to engage the Alliance anymore even when the Alliance marched into Beijing. By doing so, Li Hong Zhang again carried the name of traitor, since his interference prevented the Muslim Army to pull back from the brink of victories.

Li also defended for the Viceroys from other provinces, such Yuan Shi Kai in Shandong, and Zhang Zhi Dong in Hunan, for their disobedience to Qing Court's request to send armies to reinforce the battles in Beijing. As a result, the war did not spread to Shandong and other neighboring provinces.

After capturing Beijing, the Eight-Nation Alliance announced that the entire Beijing was under Alliance control except two residences – one was the residence of Li Hong Zhang, the other one was the residence of Prince Qingqing, who had been negotiating with the Alliance until Li arrived.

Li Hong Zhang again was the one to apologize to the foreigners for the mess created by the others. On July 17, 1900, when the seventy-seven years old Li embarked the ship to travel from Guangdong to Tianjin upon receiving the edict to ask him to negotiate with the Alliance, the Magistrate of Nanhai, Pei Jing Fu, asked him what he would do to reduce the damage to minimum, he sighed: "How I could predict? I can only do my best to pester the Alliance. How many years I have to live? Every day I live, I do my job. I only hope that I can finish my job before I die."

Like a nightmare, Li spent the last year of his life in a sorrowful mode, racing against the clock, contending the foreigners, trying to finish his job before he died.

When Li Hong Zhang returned to Tianjin, the city he had resided for more than twenty years as the Viceroy of Zhili was burned beyond recognition. What he saw saddened him beyond grief. The Viceroy Palace, where he worked and lived for twenty years, was burned to rubble.

In November 1900, Alliance officially informed Li Hong Zhang and Prince Qingqing about their first draft of the demands: punish the responsible, ban the importation of ammunition, dismantle Dagu fortification, pay indemnity, allow Alliance garrisons between Tianjin and Beijing, guarantee safety of foreigners in the region, and allow military compounds in the embassies. These demands heavily infringed Chinese sovereign. He realized that he could not single handed save the nation from disgrace.

CiXi, while in exile in Xian, was kept informed about the progress by telegrams. She was hoping every moment there was "good news." Even though CiXi was the one who created such disaster, Li would have to shield CiXi from being the "guilty one" in front of foreigners. He pretended that he needed to get approval from CiXi for every concession. He did it in order to enhance CiXi's authority. The Alliance was more than glad to comply, because by keeping CiXi in place, it guaranteed a weak China.

Once when visiting British and German Ambassadors, Li caught cold and fell sick. He did not show up for the negotiation for the next few days. The representatives of Alliance were thinking that he was using procrastination as a strategy, and made clear to Li that they were quite unhappy.

The Treaty

After the Alliance captured Beijing, the negotiation was more like for unconditional surrender. Li was weak, feeble and very old. His physical condition did not allow him to sit on the negotiation table for hours and hours, facing the unending demands from the Alliance, and at the same time, receiving contemptible critics at home. He knew that he would not live much longer. He was eager to put episode to an end as soon as possible, so was CiXi. After few months, both sides came up with an agreeable memorandum.

CiXi was grateful that the draft of memorandum did not point her as the responsible, nor asked her to give up power. She quickly sent the message to

Li to agree. On January 15, 1901, he signed the memorandum. The Chinese public opinion denounced him for the selling out of China's interest.

There were no shortages of critics. The Viceroy Zhang Zhi Dong insisted that Li should not sign the treaty under the unfavorable conditions. Li countered that without agreeing to the conditions, it would lead to the breakdown of the negotiation, and caused further wars, and there was no room for negotiation, reminding that the Alliance troops were still occupying Beijing. He was hoping to wrap up the negotiation sooner so that he could rest for whatever short time he would have. He wished that after signing the memorandum, the Alliance would withdraw the troops from Beijing. However, the Alliance had no sign of withdrawing, citing that they would not withdraw until the amount of the indemnity finalized, and the responsible persons brought to justice.

The punishment of the responsible was also a sticking point. He would not accept the humiliation of public executions of the royal families and court officials. It was especially tough for CiXi, because many of them were loyal to her.

When Yu Xian, the Viceroy of Shandong, who first sponsored the Boxers, met CiXi during exile, he had heard that the Alliance listed him as one of the responsible for execution. He begged CiXi to save his life. CiXi told him that he did a good job. However, she would have to strip all his duties and exile him to GuangXu to appease the Alliance. Yu Xian thought that with CiXi's support, finally he could escape death. He went quickly to GuangXu. However, he did not expect that the Alliance would hold him responsible for sponsoring the Boxers and kill several foreigners in Shanxi, and insisted on his death. They threatened CiXi that if he was not brought to justice, the Alliance would continue to march into interior of China. In the end, CiXi had no choice but to order his execution. When Yu Xian was apprehended in GuangXu and was brought to the execution ground, he asked, "On whose order that I will be executed?"

The executioner replied, "The order comes from Empress CiXi."

Xi Yuan seemed relieved, "I am glad that I will not die in the hands of foreigners. My head is well worth of ten foreigners' heads."

When the news of his execution arrived in Shanxi, where he had his last job as Viceroy there, people wept and remembered him as a good official.

The Alliance yielded on the execution of Prince Duan, because he was a member of the royal family. However, he was exiled to Xinjiang for life. In 1921, ten years after the fall of Qing Dynasty, he thought that it was safe for him to go back to Beijing. He sneaked back to Beijing. Unfortunately, he was discovered and under the protest of the Alliance, the police caught him and sent him back to exile again.

The amount of indemnity posted the biggest problem. Li was too exhausted to fight for better conditions. Moreover, his health was already in critical condition -he had vomited blood in several occasions. Nevertheless, Li could not forget the critics, negotiated for the best. The Alliance had demanded each ounce for each Chinese.

Li sent a letter to Qing Court, "Every time we have a treaty, every time we lose more. Now I am hopeful that the deal is almost done, and peace can be restored. I hope that the Court can appreciate the cost of the peace and keep it. Maybe there is a chance for China if we will devote ourselves to overhaul the country. "

It could be imagined how disappointed, grudgingly he must have felt to negotiate over and over for the tough conditions imposed on China.

On September 7, 1901, Li signed the treaty with Eight-Nation Alliance. China agreed to pay 450 million troy ounces as war compensation plus interest. Russia got the largest amount, 29%, Germany 20%, France 16%, Britain 11%, Japan 7.7%, U.S. 7.3%, Italy 6%, Belgium 1.9% and others less than 1%. The penalty could build Beiyang Fleet many times over. It was payable in thirty-nine years with four percent of interest. It was the largest indemnity ever for all the unequal treaties. The amount was equivalent to eleven years of Qing Court's revenue. Since China could not pay this entire amount, China agreed to concede more control of Custom to foreign powers. Part of the payment would be collected from the custom duty. Other part would be collected from tax revenues. Such a burden further impoverished the already poor China. Qing Court was stripped its entire tax revenue source. Year 1901 was the year Gengzi in Chinese calendar. The indemnity was therefore called "Indemnity of Gengzi."

In 1906, the Chancellor of the University of Illinois, Edmond James, sent a memo to the President Theodore Roosevelt to attract Chinese students to study in the U.S. In the March, same year, Arthur Henderson Smith, a priest, went to see Roosevelt and proposed to use the Gengzi Indemnity as the scholarship fund for the Chinese students to study in the U.S. On 1909, the U.S. set up the Boxer Rebellion Indemnity Scholarship Program. Under this program, the United States gradually returned her surplus portion of the indemnity to China, after paying her damage and cost of the war. The returned fund was stipulated specifically for the education of Chinese students in the universities in the U.S. In 1924, the U.S. Congress passed the motion to return the balance amount twelve million and five hundred thousand dollars of the indemnity to fund a university – the Qinghua University.

Li had negotiated for the best terms of the punishment for the responsible persons. The Manchu Viceroy Yu Xian, who was the first sponsor of the Boxers, received the death sentence, but the Alliance spared Chinese General Dong Fu Xiang. Both were anti-foreign and had encouraged the killing of foreigners during the rebellion. However, under Li's insistence, the Alliance agreed that General Dong Fu Xiang was a military commander who followed the orders. He received the punishment of the removal of all his positions and titles and the exile to his home province of Gansu. As a member of royal family, Prince Duan was sentenced to exile to Xinjiang, the remote western frontier of China with Central Asia.

Besides the indemnity, Qing Court also agreed to let the foreign powers station armies between Beijing and Tianjin, to remove all the fortifications between Tianjin and Beijing, to prohibit any anti-Western organization.

When Li returned home from signing the treaty, he was exhausted and collapsed, and was diagnosed having terminal disease. He was seventy-eight years old. The pressure and hard work that he took debilitated him completely.

However, two months after Qing Court signed the treaty with the Alliance countries, Russian government wanted to renegotiate for more concessions. At that time, Li was already bedridden, could not even walk. The Russian envoy visited Li at home and forced him to amend the treaty. When he saw that Li was dying at his last gasp, he was leaving. Moments later, Li breathed his last exhalation, the servants cried, and the Russian envoy turned around. Li suddenly opened his eyes, saying, "I cannot give you anymore...," then he passed away.

He wrote a letter to CiXi in his deathbed: "I had spent my life to serve Qing, and Your Highness. I am sorry that I have to go now. There is so much more I want to do, but cannot do anymore. After one defeat after another, China was badly hurt. People cannot make a living in this kind of impoverished state much longer. I wish that Your Highness would be successful in putting this country in order, to build a peaceful and prosperous China. In order to do so, Your Highness will have to make peace with foreigners. Then I will have no more regret."

On November 7, 1901, he died with remaining grievance. When CiXi received the news, she cried, "No one else can share my burden anymore!"

After his death, CiXi conferred him several honorable titles, and built memorial halls for him throughout China.

Chinese Mercenaries

The events of war were highly reported by both Chinese journalists and the Western media. Clearly, a large part of Western victories was not due to their military prowess. Many Chinese soldiers fought very bravely. China could have mobilized many more manpower to fight the war.

Ironically, included in the Eight-Nation Alliance Army, there were also brigades consisting mostly Chinese mercenaries, under British and German commanders. The British recruited their Chinese soldiers from Weihaiwei and Hong Kong, trained them in Britain, while the German recruited their Chinese mercenaries from Qingdao, the city recently leased to Germany.

In 1899, German established a company of Chinese soldiers called "Chinese Brave Company" or Hua Yong Company in Qingdao. The company belonged to the third battalion of Marine. The German prince Heinrich valued this company highly after his inspection.

The British Chinese Mercenary Battalion was formed in Weihaiwei, which had been leased to Britain not long ago. British colonies were around the world. Its military resources were spreading very thin. Britain employed many mercenaries in her army. Britain started to organize the Chinese mercenary troop in November 1898. The organizers did not realize that to serve in military was not an honorable profession in China, especially to serve in the military of foreign powers. They had difficult time in recruiting. By March 1899, they recruited only ten mercenaries. The Germans faced the same difficulty. In addition, the recruited mercenaries were much undisciplined. They would leave the garrison without reporting, or quit after a while. Some simply vanished. It had been a problem in the Chinese army in general. The lack of discipline and training was one of the reasons that the Chinese armies could not fight in many instances.

Soon, they changed the strategy. They paid high salaries, and targeted the ex-soldiers who had served in the Qing Army. The new recruits were easier to train and familiar with the military operation.

By May 1900, the British Chinese mercenary battalion had a force of five hundred men, mostly between twenty three to twenty five years old. The battalion was well equipped: It had rifle company, machine gun company, cannon regiment and cavalry regiment all equipped with the best weaponries the British army had.

The mercenary contract was for three years. Their mission could be anywhere in the world. Every day, there were five hours of training. Very soon, their quality as a fighting force was greatly elevated. British commander exclaimed, "If the Qing Court could train them like this, we would not be able to win even one war."

British officer Arthur Barnes published a journal in 1902 entitled: "On Active Service with The Chinese Regiment : A Record of The Operation of The First Chinese Regiment in North China from March to October 1900" described in detail how this brave mercenary regiment fought. The Chinese Regiment made major contribution to put down the revolt of Weihaiwei local people against the British occupation from March through June 1900.

On June 22, 1900, the British First Chinese Regiment with two hundred men and ten officers arrived in Dagu fortification by British warship Orlando. One day before, another regiment from Hong Kong with four hundred men had arrived. This was in addition to the Chinese Regiment from Singapore. These three regiments behaved bravely in the Eight-Nation Alliance War.

A No Win War for China

China lost the war not without putting a fight. In many occasions, the Chinese troops fought brilliantly and bravely, and defeated the Alliance troops. However, the quality of the Chinese troops was very inconsistent. While the Muslim Braves under General Dong fought fiercely, the Manchu Bannermen Division under Prince Duan's command was a disaster.

Prince Duan himself neither knew how to command a troop, nor knew anything about battle strategy. His own Manchu Bannermen Division also called the "Tiger Spirit Division," had 10,000 men. It was one of the three modernized Manchu Banner Divisions. The troop was totally wasted under his command. Prince Duan also misled CiXi in believing that the Boxers were a defense force. In reality, they were a disorderly and riotous crowd of people. Even when Muslim Army integrated them, they did not receive any military training. They could not function as an army.

However, the most damaging effect was from the mixed Chinese emotion towards the war. On one hand, it was a defense against invasion. On the other hand, there was lack of confidence that China was no match to the Western Powers and soon or later China would lose. Therefore, China wanted fight like patriot and at the same time was afraid of fighting would infuriate Western Powers even more. China was torn between "can fight" and "cannot fight."

Many things that Qing Court did were knowingly to give the Alliance an upper hand to win. For example, before the official declaration of war, both sides knew that the war was imminent. Yet, Qing Court allowed the Alliance troops to use the railroad to transport its troop freely to Beijing, an unthinkable action for the warring states.

Rong Lu and Prince Qingqing never gave up negotiating with the Alliance during the war, and consciously undercut the effort of the Imperial Army in the defense between Tianjin and Beijing. When Dong Fu Xiang's Muslim troops were eager to and could have stopped the Alliance troops from advancing, Rong Lu prevented him from doing so by denying them the critical military supplies.

The battle of Yangcun was the last battle of the war. However, Chinese army was willingly giving up the defense. Rong Lu retrieved the troops after initial confrontation. Yangcun was only half way between Tianjin and Beijing. The Chinese troops were still intact to fight for further defense. If Rong Lu had resolved to fight, the Chinese Army could have well defeated the Alliance troop the second time. The defeat of the Alliance's second expedition would certainly make the Alliance to reconsider their positions. Either they would launch a third expedition with much larger force or they would accept a condition in favor of Chinese.

The Last Days of An Empire

The Siege of Legation also demonstrated the Chinese dilemma between "wanting to fight" and "being afraid to lose". Initially, when Prince Duan issued an edict to attack the Legation, Rong Lu feigned the attack by firing firecrackers. Only when the foreigners in the Legations, without knowing the attack was real or not, killed the messenger of ceasefire, and opened fire on Dong Fu Xiang's army, and forced the Muslim army to return fire, the siege became real.

Even during the siege, Rong Lu and Prince Qingqing continued to send food supplies to the Legation, order the protection of foreigners and in occasions, sabotage the Muslim Gansu Braves to prevent the siege from out of control.

As Rong Lu and Li Hong Zhang were both very old and very ill, they did not have the will to fight. Their lack of confidence led them to ignore the fact that they could have negotiated a better deal under strength rather than weakness. Their outlook of their own life affected tremendously the fate of China.

Furthermore, due to the nature of the Boxer, many intellectuals, high government officers, and business community considered the Boxers as mob. They needed to be terminated, not helped. They were appalled by the fact that Qing Court even supported them. Even inside of Qing Court, the support of the Boxer was not unanimous. Emperor GuangXu himself did not have the sympathy on the Boxers. China was torn also between "should fight" and "should not fight."

When the Boxers first arrived in Tianjin and Beijing early 1900, driven out of Shandong by Yuan Shi Kai, they were not welcome. Qing Court was afraid of their disturbance, and ordered their arrest and blocked more of them from entering the cities. They were outlaws until Prince Duan took the advantage and used them to instigate the attack on foreigners. Once the Boxers were encouraged by Prince Duan, they came in large numbers and their behavior became more audacious.

Prince Duan provoked the war deliberately out of his hatred of the foreigners. He ordered the Boxers to burn churches, kill foreigners, ransack foreign compounds and destroy railroads. Many Chinese were outraged by Prince Duan's orders. They did not want to side with the Prince Duan's evil intention and CiXi's ignorance. Although the barbarous acts by the Alliance soldiers also angered many Chinese. Even after the declaration of the war, Qing Court could not bring herself to be coordinated with unified front to fight the war. Were the Boxers patriots or mobs? There was no agreement.

Several Manchu princes, such as Prince Qingqing declined to join the Boxers and attack the Legations, and even ordered their own Manchu Bannermen to attack the Boxers and the Muslim Kansu braves.

After Prince Duan officially sanctioned the Boxers, conflicting orders came. Rong Lu's order to General Nie to protect the railroad put him in direct confrontation with the Boxers, who were sabotaging the railroad. While protected the railroad, General Nie could not prevent the Alliance from using it to transport their troops into Tianjin from Dagu. Fighting the Boxers also tied down thousands of General Nie troops, which was already outnumbered by the Alliance troop. Under such inept command, when Tianjin fell, General Nie decided to take his own life by walking into the range of Allied guns.

The rivalries between the Boxers and the Chinese Imperial Army were playing tug of war. Conflicting orders caused the loss of many opportunities to win the battles. This resulted in the Chinese forces calculatingly letting the Alliance forces escape, after the Chinese encircled them at the Battle of LangFang.

China had the psychology of no win. Such a psychology prevented China from fighting the war for long. Chinese psychology was as a personality split. It inflicted damage onto itself.

The Alliance was confused at first, however was quick to take advantages of Qing Court's indecision and played rivalries against each other. The Alliance put pressure on Prince Qingqing and Li Hong Zhang, through Rong Lu, to undermine Chinese fighting forces in the field. Despite the fact that the Alliance consisted of eight nations, nevertheless, they had strategy that is more coherent and unified goals in this war.

Chapter 5

Open Door Policy

The great powers stopped short of finally colonizing China. From the Boxer rebellions, they learned that the best way to govern China was through the Chinese dynasty, instead of direct dealing with the Chinese people. The popular saying was "The people are afraid of officials, the officials are afraid of foreigners, and the foreigners are afraid of the people"

There was no advantage of colonizing China, if the foreign powers could extract the economic advantages from China as they already had. CiXi was allowed to stay in power, since CiXi's reign guaranteed a weak China.

However, there were two exceptions: Russia and Japan. Because of their geographic proximity to China, they could gain more advantage by territorial claims.

In 1898, the United States had enhanced her power in East Asia through the colonization of the Philippine. When the partition of China by the European powers and Japan seemed imminent, the United States felt its commercial interests in China threatened. The U.S. Secretary of State John Hay issued a statement to the major powers having interests in China, asking them to declare formally that they would uphold Chinese territorial and administrative integrity and would not interfere with the free use of the treaty ports within their spheres of influence in China.

In reply, each nation tried to evade Hay's request, taking the position that it could not commit itself until the other nations had complied. However, by July 1900, Hay announced that each of the powers had granted consent in principle. Although treaties made after 1900 refer to the Open Door Policy, competition among the various powers for special concessions within China for railroad rights, mining rights, loans, foreign trade ports, and so forth, continued unabated.

In October 1900, Russia continued to move their troops to occupy Manchuria. Their move threatened other powers' hope of maintaining China's territorial integrity.

In 1902, the United States government protested that Russian encroachment in Manchuria was a violation of the Open Door Policy, but not much was done. Soon, the Japan took the matter in their hands.

Among the Imperial powers, Japan gained most prestige to be part of the Eight-Nation Alliance, and was recognized as a power equal to the other Western Powers. It encouraged greatly her ambition and audacity. Japan would not tolerate for long that its prey, the Manchuria, taken by someone else.

Russian Occupation

By the end of the nineteenth century, Russia was already the country with the largest continuous landmass from Poland in the west to the Kamchatka peninsula in the East. However, she did not stop her expansion, especially toward East Asia. From 1858 until the end of Qing Dynasty in 1911, China signed five treaties with Russia conceding 800,000 square miles of territories, about the size of Alaska and California combined. However, Russia was not satisfied. Tsar Nicholas II openly claimed Russian ambition: "Russia wants a warm water port which could be used year around, and this port has to be on the continuous extension of Russian territory." The only place such ports existed is Korea and China. Tsar' s ambition eventually costed his own life and his dynasty.

To overcome the distance from Russia Europe, Russia built a Trans Siberia Railroad in the 1890's. The then prince Nicholas II personally went to Vladivostok to preside over the groundbreaking ceremony in 1891. Russian Finance Minister Sergey Julevich Vitte claimed that after the railroad was built, Russia would be able to project her military power in the shortest time to Far East.

However, the Maguan Treaty that China signed with Japan in 1894 was a severe blow to Russian's ambition. Immediately, Russia intervened. Qing

Court naively thought that Russia was helping China. China paid Japan additional 30 million taels of silver for Japan to give up her rights in Manchuria. In less than two years, Russia coerced China into signing another treaty to transfer the rights that Japan gave up to Russia. In March 1897, Russia got what she wanted: the right to build railroad, with freedom of transport her troops in Manchuria and the lease of Port Arthur. By the end of 1897, Russian Fleet not only anchored in Port Arthur, but also physically occupied it. They lost no time in fortifying Port Arthur, their sole warm-water port on the Pacific coast, and of great strategic value. A year later, in order to consolidate their position, the Russians began a new railway from Harbin through Mukden, also known as Shenyang, to Port Arthur. The Russians also began to make inroads into Korea; by 1898, they acquired mining and forestry concessions near Yalu and Tumen rivers, causing the Japanese much anxiety.

During the Eight-Nation Alliance invasion, Russia took the advantage to physically occupying Manchuria. When the Eight-Nation Alliance withdrew their troops from China one year after the invasion, Russian troops, numbering 180,000 men, remained in Manchuria.

The Japanese Prime Minister Ito Hirobumi started to negotiate with the Russians. Meanwhile, Japan and Britain had signed the Anglo-Japanese Alliance Agreement in 1902. Britain sought to restrict naval competition by keeping the Port Arthur from the exclusive use by Russia. The alliance with the Britain meant, in part, that if any nation allied itself with Russia during any war with Japan, then Britain would enter the war on Japan's side. Britain's intention was to prevent Russia from allying herself to either Germany or France. With the Anglo-Japanese Alliance Agreement, Russia could no longer count on receiving help from either Germany or France without there being a danger of the British involvement in the event of a war. With such an alliance, Japan applied more pressure to Russia. The Anglo-Japanese Alliance eventually proved to be a major setback when the Russian Baltic Fleet traveled six months without being able to replenish in the French controlled Cam Ranh Bay in Vietnam.

Under international pressure, Russia signed a treaty with China on April 8, 1902, agreeing to withdraw the troop and to return the railroad right to China within 18 months. However, Russia did not intent to give up its conquered gains. After symbolic withdraw, Russia stepped up to set up a Viceroy Office for Far East to oversee the occupation.

During this period, Russia worked hard to penetrate and exert influence to every corner of Manchuria. She had built over hundred thirty churches and four hundred schools, numerous newspapers and magazines, many associations and institutes followed by a large number of Russian immigrants. Under the cover of scientific research, Russia dispatched pioneers with diversified background, e.g. engineers, geologists, disguised military personnel, and botanist, to uncover the nature resources, economic potentials, topography and terrains in Manchuria. The research reports laid a foundation for the eventual occupation and preparation for war.

Irritated Japan

Since the Jiawu Sino-Japanese War, Japan had considered Manchuria as her prey. Russia's aggressive occupation raised high anxiety among Japanese politicians an military alike. Japan spent the indemnity that she received from China mostly in the military build-up. Such a build-up by 1903, according to Japanese internal consensus, was sufficient to encounter Russia in Manchuria. The voices to stop Russia's further advance in Manchuria was unbridled.

Seeing that Russians did not step down their activities in Manchuria, on July 28, 1903, the Japanese Ambassador in St. Petersburg presented to Tsar his country's view opposing Russia's consolidation plans in Manchuria. On August 12, the Japanese minister handed proposed the terms and conditions for further negotiations.

Japan, following Prime Minister Ito Hirobumi's thinking, was willing to recognize Russia's gain in Manchuria in exchange of Russian recognition of Japan's rights in Korea. However, the Russians essentially saw Korea as a buffer between Russia and Japan. Although Russia was willing to recognize Japan's interest in Korea, however, she wanted to restrict Japanese military activities in Korea, without limiting her military activities in Manchuria. When the Russian Ambassador to Japan, Roman Rosen, submitted the counter proposal to Japan on October 3, the negotiation broke down.

Tsar Nicholas II deliberately provoked Japanese because he misjudged that the war against Japan would spark Russian patriotism and therefore would alleviate his domestic pressure. He also unwisely predicted that Japan would not go to war due to Russia's far larger and seemingly superior Navy and Army. In addition, he further believed that if Japan were going to the war, Russia could defeat Japan easily just as she defeated China. Russian

General Alexei Kuropatkin boosted, after visiting Japan in 1902: "One Russian soldier could fight three Japanese soldiers. We need only two weeks to group a troop of four-hundred-thousand-manpower in Manchuria." He claimed that if Japan launched the war, he would not only defeat Japan in Manchuria but also launch an attack on Japan proper and capture the Japanese emperor. Alexei Kuropatkin largely convinced Tsar Nicholas II against the opinions from other advisors. Many of his advisors did not share this view and foreseeing difficulties in transporting troops and supplies from European Russia to the East.

From Japanese point of view, they were patient enough and made sufficient concession to give up her rights in Manchuria, and yet what Russian wanted was more than fair deal. To the Japanese, the only way that they could gain what they wanted was through a war.

Japan figured out that Russian main fighting force was in Europe. It would take long to arrive in Far East; especially not the entire Trans-Siberia Railroad was ready. If they could launch a surprising and devastating attack to destroy Russian Far East Fleet, therefore, control the Yellow Sea, Japan could then transport the troops to Korea without resistance. Japanese troop could quickly advance to Manchuria and annihilate the Russian troops there, before any reinforcement from Europe could arrive. Once the strategy was plotted out, Japan moved quickly.

On February 6, 1904, the Japanese Ambassador to Russia, Kurino Shichiro, informed the Russian Foreign Minister, Count Lambsdorff that he was recalled back to Japan. On the same day, Japan severed diplomatic relations with Russia. Two days later, on February 8, 1904, Japan declared the war on Russia and launched a surprise attack on Russian Far East Fleet at Port Arthur even before the Russian government had received the declaration of war.

Interestingly enough, Japan used the same strategy to attack the U.S. in the Pearl Harbor thirty-seven years later.

Tsar Nicholas II was stunned by news of the attack. He could not believe that Japan would commit an act of war without a formal declaration. Russia declared war on Japan eight days later.

The strategy of the Russian Far East Fleet was to use Port Arthur to control the Yellow Sea and the Korean Strait, preventing Japanese troop to land in Korea, and attacking Japan from two sides by battleships from Vladivostok in one direction and from Port Arthur in the other direction. By cutting off Japanese reinforcement, Russian troop could easily move into Korea and holding Korea to fend off Japanese aggression. Strategically, it made sense. However, in the winters, Port Vladivostok could not be used. Therefore, most of the battleships of the Russian Far East Fleet were anchored in Port Arthur in the winter.

Battle of Yalu River

The Imperial Russian Army fortified Port Arthur into a major naval base since its occupation in 1896. Controlling the railroad in Manchuria, Russia could easily access Port Arthur just like Vladivostok. Since Port Arthur is a warm water port, which can be used year around, Russia had moved most of her Far East Fleet into Port Arthur in the winter season, which would be proven a deadly mistake.

On the night of February 8, 1904, the Japanese fleet under Admiral Togo Heihachiro attacked the Russian ships with torpedo from destroyers at Port Arthur unexpectedly. The attack badly damaged two of the heaviest battleships in Russia's Far Eastern Fleet, and a 6,600-ton cruiser. The Battle of Port Arthur started.

While the Russians were too oblivious of the Japanese naval activities in the Far East, the Japanese success was largely due to the element of surprise. After the initial attack, the Russians immediately protect the remaining battleships by their shore batteries. As a result, Admiral Togo was unable to attack the Russian Fleet successfully again with further naval engagements.

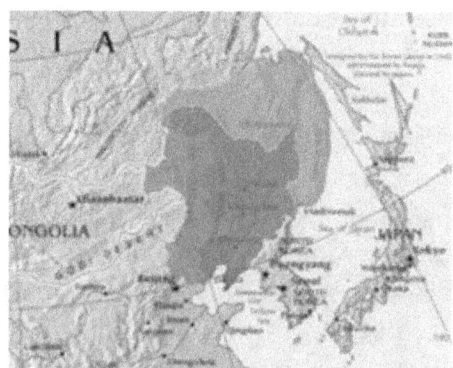

Figure 16 The Grand Manchuria

The second Japanese strategy was to blockade Russian ships from leaving the port by implanting deep-water mines in the channel to the port. On April 12, 1904, two Russian battleships were unaware of the mines, slipped out of port and struck Japanese mines. One sank almost immediately, while the other had to be towed back to port for extensive repairs. Admiral Makarov, a highly regarded Russian naval strategist, perished on the battleship.

Since then, Russian battleships were kept from venturing out to leave the harbor for the open seas. By doing so, the entire fleet became useless.

After gaining control of the sea between Korea and China, Japan soon landed more troops near Incheon in Korea, and moved them northward. By the end of April, the Imperial Japanese Army under Kuroki Itei was ready to move cross the Yulu River, the natural border between China and Korea, into Russian-occupied Manchuria.

The unexpected Japanese attack caught Russia by surprise. She had not had the time to mobilize her main troops in European Russia into Far East. Therefore, Russian tried to procrastinate to gain time for reinforcements to arrive via the Trans-Siberia Railway, which had not been fully completed yet.

At that time, Russia had Eastern Detachment of 20,000 men stationed in the north side of Yalu River, or the Chinese side. Southern Detachment of 22,000 men stationed at YingKou. The Russian Guangdong Detachment of 30,000 men stationed near Port Arthur, and a main division of 30,000 men stationed at Liaoyang. In addition, there was a division of 30,000 men strong stationed in the Russian Far East near Vladivostok, a total force about 132,000 men in the Far East. It was a considerable force, not to mention that the reinforcement was arriving from Europe soon.

On the other side of the Yalu River, Japanese troop commanded by General Tamemoto Kuroki outnumbered Russian Eastern Detachment, under the command of Lieutenant-General Mikhail Zasulich, by two to one. Due to the lack of military intelligence, the Russian army did not know where the Japanese troop would cross the river; therefore, General Zasulich spread his manpower over 170 miles long along the Yalu River.

Only ten years earlier, Japan had won the battle against Qing Dynasty also at Yalu River, Japanese army was familiar with the terrain, knew the area well. By April 21, 1904, the Japanese first Army was concentrated in the south side of Yalu River, or the Korean side, near Wiju. Japanese knew the exact locations of the Russians deployment from intelligence by forward scouts disguised as Korean anglers. By April 23, Japanese knew the layout the Russian trench line and details of the defensive positions around the area of Andong, the largest city along the Yalu River. The Japanese made every effort keep their positions hidden.

On the night of April 25, 1904, two battalions of the Japanese Division seized two small islands in the Yalu River without opposition. After a brief firefight, the Russian observation post withdrew to the main Russian lines on the north shore.

By the time when the Battle of Yalu River started, the Russian army had yet to finish the defense construction since they only arrived less than one month earlier. It was forced to fight head-on with the larger force of the Japanese army.

General Kuroki planned to attack the upper stream of Yalu River because the river was narrower and shallower. It was easier for his troop to cross. However, he ordered a feint on the downstream of the river using Japanese gunboats to engage Russian troops at the river mouth. This convinced General Zasulich that the Japanese would attack the vicinity of Andong, which was only ten miles from the Yalu River mouth. Therefore, he concentrated his forces there. General Kuroki's distraction plan worked.

Meanwhile, General Kuroki deployed his troop across the upper stream of Yalu River against the weak points of the Russian defense on the other side of the river. Japanese quickly constructed several causeway bridges at a fordable point across the River. Even though Zasulitch received reports of Japanese activities there, he remained convinced that the main Japanese attack would fall at Andong, and kept his main force as well as his reserves there.

The Japanese attack began in the dawn of April 27, 1904. By then, majority of Japanese troops of over 30,000 men had already crossed the river using the causeway bridges without much resistance, and was advancing in three columns. The weather also helped the Japanese. Limited visibility masked the Japanese movements from Russian observation. When the fog finally lifted, the Japanese artillery of the right column opened up on the Russian formations in the north.

The center column advanced and caught the Russians artillery division in a claw formation on the north side of the Yalu River not far from the crossing point. Russians were surprised at the attack and were outnumbered. When Russians retreated, Japanese attempted to block their escape towards the north.

The Japanese had a number of heavy howitzers, which devastated the exposed Russians. When General Zasulitch realized Japanese strategy, he wanted to pull back to a more defensible position. However, without admitting his mistake, the general still sent a telegram to Tsar Nicholas II informing that victory was guaranteed.

General Kuroki had planned to continue the advance to envelope the Russian left. However, now the Japanese troop had neutralized the enemy artillery, he decided to engage the column on the left, the 2nd Division, in a simultaneous assault. It was at this point the Japanese encountered the first serious resistance from the main Russian force. The Russians had successfully disrupted the advance of the second Division for a brief period. However, the Japanese drove Russian from their trenches with severe losses, and the survivors fell back to the tops of the hills. During the retreat, the Russian 12th East Siberian Rifle Regiment made a failed counter attack. The Regiment was dispersed over an extended defense line. Therefore, Russian lines opened a crack.

The Russian position now became vulnerable. Not only the long line along the Yalu River became indefensible, but also the main force near Andong was in danger of being encircled. General Zasulich ordered to retreat. The 11th East Siberian Rifle Regiment, which was covering a retreat, was cut off by the Japanese and suffered heavy casualties. When the Japanese 12th Division attacked the Russian left flank, the troop panicked and collapsed.

By the end of May 1, 1904, remnants of the Russian Eastern Detachment either surrendered or escaped to the north and the Battle of the Yalu River was over.

Siege of Port Arthur

The Battle of the Yalu River ended in victory for Japan. The defeat of the Russian Eastern Detachment dispelled the myth that the Japanese could be easily defeated just like China, and that only the Western nations could be world-class power.

Japanese army, after winning the battle, moved in two directions, one to northwest in the direction of Mukden, also known as Shenyang, the capital of Manchuria, where was heavily defended by Russians, and the other, to southwest, in the direction of Port Arthur.

While the Japanese reinforcement troop continued to come by land from Korea, other Japanese troops by sea landed at several points on the Manchurian coast, which Japan was able to do without resistance from the sea. In a series of engagements, Japanese troop drove the Russians back in two fronts between Port Arthur and Mukden. The subsequent battles, including the Battle of Nanshan on May 25, 1904, were brutal and Japan had suffered heavy losses. However, the breakthrough came for the Japanese in two decisive land battles: In late August, the Battle of Liaoyang, a city mid way between Port Arthur and Mukden, and in September, the battle of Sahe, further north of Liaoyang. Japan won both battles. As a result, Japan achieved the strategic goal that she wanted –to cut off completely the Russian reinforcement to Port Arthur by October 1904.

At Port Arthur, the Russians Navy learned quickly from the Japanese to lay the deep-sea mines. On May 15, 1904, two Japanese battleships were lured into a recently laid Russian minefield off Port Arthur, each striking at least two mines. One battleship sank within minutes, taking 450 sailors with her, while the other also sank half way undertow towards Korea for repairs.

However, Japanese troop gained upper hand in the land battle, and was approaching Port Arthur from the north. The northern Russian force, that would be to relieve Port Arthur, retreated to Mukden. Therefore, Russian reinforcement troops to relieve the besieged city, Port Arthur, by land also failed. The Russians in the Port Arthur became completely isolated. The pressure increased for Russian Fleet.

Russian Fleet now under the command of Admiral Wilgelm Vitgeft attempted a desperate breakout on August 10. However, when the fleet reached the open sea, it encountered Japanese battleship squadron commanded by Admiral Togo. The Russian and Japanese battleships exchanged fire. Unfortunately, for the Russians, the Russian flagship, Tsesarevich, was hit on the bridge. The hit instantly killed the fleet commander, Admiral Vitgeft. The Russian Fleet hastily turned around and headed back into Port Arthur. Though either side in the battle sank no warships, the Russians were now driven back to the port. The Japanese battleships guarded the entrance to the port intensively.

Shortly afterwards, Japanese intensified its attack, and began a long siege of Port Arthur with total force of 60,000 men. She had intended to take Port Arthur, and therefore, would in position to annihilate or capture all the Russian warships in the port, before Russian Baltic Fleet reinforcement arrived.

As the siege of Port Arthur continued, Japanese troops tried numerous frontal assaults on the fortified hilltops overlooking the harbor. Russians defended their hilltops sturdily, and drove back the Japanese attack with heavy casualties in the thousands. Both sides were in stalemate for couple of months. Eventually, the ammunition supply for the Russian army was winding down, and Japanese reinforcement kept coming.

With the aid of several batteries of 11-inch Krupp cannons, Japanese finally captured a key hilltop bastion in December 1904. From this vantage point, the long-range artillery was able to shell the Russian warships in the harbor. It was difficult for the Russian warship to counter attack effectively against the land-based artillery. The hilltop bastions were also much more fortified than the warships in the open. The warships were also unable to sortie out against the blockading Japanese Fleet. Any hit the warships received reduced their combat capability. The more they waited, the worse the situation became, when the Japanese were taking Russian batteries one by one.

Without the land batteries' protection, and without being able to move on to open sea, the Russian battleships became a sitting duck. The situation for Russians in Port Arthur was quite desperate. They could not hope the reinforcement from the north by land, or the reinforcement from the south by sea. The much talked about reinforcement of the Baltic Fleet had departed from the Baltic Sea only in October after much undesirable delay. It would take another six months to arrive. There was little chance that Port Arthur could hold on that long because Japanese continued to increase their force, and was assaulting Port Arthur from all directions. Four Russian battleships and two cruisers were sunk in succession, with the fifth and last battleship being forced to scuttle a few weeks later. Thus, all major battleships of the Russian Fleet in the Pacific were sunk. One of the three Russian Fleets was annihilated.

Major General Anatoly Stessel, commander of the Port Arthur garrison, realized that there was no way out of the desperate situation; he decided to surrender to the Japanese on January 2, 1905 against the wishes of his military staffs. Stessel was later convicted in 1908 and sentenced to death for his incompetent defense and treason, though he was later pardoned.

Battle of Mukden

Russians also lost ground at the land battles. Although, Russians gained some small victories and were able to recover some defensive lines at huge costs, it did not change the direction of major events. Each time, Japanese attack inflicted heavy casualties to the Russian defense troop.

After their capture of Sahe and Liaoyang in the previous year, Japanese troops moving northward met no resistance. With the onset of the severe Manchurian winter, there had been no major land engagements for a while. With the capture of Port Arthur after Russian Fleet surrender, Japan freed her troops to move northward and join the other Japanese troops in the south of Russian-held Mukden.

Figure 17 Retreat of Russian troops near Mukden

By January 1905, two sides encountered at the Southside of Mukden, where the last Russian stronghold was. Both sides camped opposite each other along a sixty miles long front lines waiting for the major battle to erupt.

When the weather finally cleared late January, from January 25 to 29, the Russian Second Army under General Oskar Sandepu launched a major offense, and almost broke through the Japanese defense line. However, without sufficient support, the attack stalled. General Oskar Ferdinand Kazimirovich Grippenberg, the inexperienced newly arrived commanding general of the Russian Second Manchurian Army, was ordered to halt by Commander Kuropatkin and the stalemate did not end until Japanese launched an all-out counter offense on February 20, thus started the Battle of Mukden. The Battle of Mukden was the most decisive land battle in the Russo-Japanese War. On the Japanese side, there were 250,000 men, over 1,000 artillery pieces and on the Russia side, there were 285,000 men over 1,300 artillery pieces, including some newly arrived reinforcement from Europe after several months of travel. It was a large-scale warfare. The front stretched sixty miles long.

On February 23, the Japanese troop, moving northward, launched an attack on the right flank of the Russian troop. Russian commander Kuropatkin dispatched his left flank to reinforce the right flank. Unexpectedly, the attack on the right flank was a camouflage. The main Japanese force was going to attack the left flank of the Russian troop. When commander Kuropatkin realized it, he quickly recalled the reinforcement. The reinforcement troop ran back and forth in an exhaustive maneuver.

Before the reinforcement could return, Japanese troops already instigated an all-out assault on the left flank. It had two corps against one corp of Russian troop.

Commander Kuropatkin ordered his troop to retreat in order to join the reinforcement on its way back and decided to launch a counter attack to fend off the Japanese. However, he made another misjudgment. His large counter attack force encountered a small Japanese force without realizing that the Japanese troop cut off its way to retreat. Soon the Russian troop was surrounded.

After the Japanese army scattered the left flank of the Russian troop, many divisions were starting to retreat northward. The formation of the Russian troop was broken. The scattered Russian troops met with highly concentrated Japanese troops, and suffered huge causalities. When Russian troops failed to regroup, Japanese troops move around the city on the outer peripheral and controlled major roads going all directions. Seeing they were about to be encircled, the Russians began a general retreat, fighting a series of fierce rearguard skirmishes. Without being able to use the roads, it further slowed down the Russian troop movement. The situation was confusing, difficult to control, and soon caused the collapse of Russian forces. On March 10, 1905 after three weeks of intense battles with heavy losses, General Kuropatkin decided to withdraw to the north of Mukden.

The retreating Russian Army formations disbanded as fighting units. However, the Japanese themselves also had suffered heavy casualties and could not pursue further. Although the battle of Mukden was a major defeat for the Russians it was decisive as the land battle, but the outcome was still undecided because the Baltic Fleet was yet to come. The final victory could still depend on the navy. If the Baltic Fleet could annihilate the Japanese Fleet, it could recapture the Port Arthur. By then, more reinforcement troop transported by the Trans-Siberia Railroad could also arrive. The Japanese army would then be surrounded from both north and south. At the same time, without the Japanese Fleet, the Baltic Fleet would control the Yellow Sea, therefore, preventing any further Japanese troop from Japan to arrive in Manchuria. The war could still turn in favor of the Russians. Therefore, all hopes were pinned on the Baltic Fleet.

The fleet was Russia's best and was under Admiral Zinovy Petrovich Rozhestvensky. It sailed around the world from the Baltic Sea to China via the Cape of Good Hope. The trip took seven months and the fleet arrived in Far East by May 1905. By that time, the Port Arthur battle had long been finished. Even the land battles had ceased after the Russian complete retreat from Mukden.

Battle of Tsushima

The Russian Baltic Fleet sailed around the world to Far East for the most critical mission. Prevented from using the Suez Canal by the British, the Russian Baltic Fleet had to take the voyage around the Cape of Good Hope, a trip of 18,000 miles. Japan derived from the Anglo-Japanese alliance pact a major benefit.

When the Baltic Fleet arrived in Madagascar, several battleships from the Russian Black Sea Fleet joined the Baltic Fleet. The combined fleet was renamed as the Russian Second Pacific Squadron. The demoralizing news that Port Arthur had fallen to Japanese reached the fleet while at Madagascar. Port Arthur would be no longer available to the Russian Fleet. The crew's moral was already low before receiving the news of Russian defeat in Port Arthur and Manchuria; it was even lower after the news arrived.

After long travel, Baltic Fleet badly needed to replenish. According to the International Convention, the neutral country could not provide anchoring to the warring country in her port. Therefore, for the seven months voyage, the Baltic Fleet had not anchored at any port. To sustain such long trip, the ships were fully loaded with coal, even on the decks, whose weight further slow down the speed. The crewmembers were all exhausted after months of traveling in the tropical sea with rationed water. The heat inside of cabins was unbearable.

Not only that majority of the ports that it could use were all controlled by Britain, but also the France and Germany, as friendly states to Russia would not help. When the Russian Second Pacific Squadron joined with the smaller Russian Third Pacific Squadron in Cam Ranh Bay in Vietnam, it requested French permission to anchor at the Bay, since France was on friendly term with Russia. However, after strong Japanese protest, France refused Russian's request. Germany occupied Qingdao port was nearby, she was also unwilling to risk her relationship with Japan.

Admiral Rozhestvensky's only hope now was to reach the port of Vladivostok. The shortest route passed directly through Korean Strait between Korea and Japan, which was in enemy's turf. It was too risky for the Russian Second Pacific Squadron. However, the other routes required the fleet to contour the entire Japan archipelago, adding additional 2000 miles to the trip, which would take two more weeks. Under the circumstances, Admiral Rozhestvensky decided that it was not an option. He would take the risk.

Admiral Togo was aware of Russian progress and understood that with the fall of Port Arthur, the Second Pacific Squadrons could anchor at the only other Russian port in the Far East, Vladivostok. He laid down the Battle plans and repaired the ships and wait for the Russian Fleet to arrive.

The Japanese fleet, which had originally consisted of six battleships, was now down to four, but retained its cruisers, destroyers, and torpedo boats. The Russian Fleet contained eight battleships, as well as cruisers, destroyers and other auxiliaries for 38 ships. It was a formidable force.

By the end of May the Russian Fleet, taking the shorter, riskier route through Korea Strait between Korea and Japan, and travelling at night to avoid discovery. By doing so, Admiral Rozhestvensky had committed a fatal mistake. It would be less disastrous if the Russian Second Pacific Squadron had traveled through during the day and encountered the Japanese fleet face to face. An all-out battle was not necessarily in Japan's favor.

However, by traveling at night, the Russian Fleet could not avoid the detection by Japanese fleet. The Japanese positioned the fleet in "the Cross the T," or vertically, against the Russian Fleet. In such position, the Russian battleships became much larger targets than the Japanese ships. After nearly one day of fierce battle, the Japanese fleet virtually annihilated the Russian Fleet, which lost the entire eight heavy battleships, numerous smaller vessels, and nearly 5,000 men. Only three Russian battleships managed to escape. The total lost tonnage was 270,000 tons – a world record that was not broken for many years. On the other hand, the Japanese lost only 3 torpedo boats and 116 men. It was the largest sea battle disaster that world had ever seen. Only three Russian vessels escaped to Vladivostok.

Military and civilian observers worldwide closely followed the course of the war. The defeats of the Russian Army and Navy shook Russian confidence. Throughout 1905, the Imperial Russian government was rocked by revolution. Tsai Nicholas II was overwhelmed by the domestic strive that he did not have the energy and attention to fight Japanese more.

The U.S. President Theodore Roosevelt offered to mediate, and earned a Nobel Peace Prize for his effort. Sergius Witte led the Russian delegation and Komura, a graduate of Harvard, led the Japanese Delegation. Both sides signed the Treaty of Portsmouth on September 5, 1905, at the Portsmouth Naval Shipyard in Kittery, Maine.

After courting the Japanese, Roosevelt decided to support the Tsar's refusal to pay indemnities, a move that policymakers in Tokyo interpreted as signifying that the United States had more than a passing interest in Asian affairs. Russia recognized Korea as part of the Japanese sphere of influence and agreed to evacuate Manchuria.

Russia signed over its 25-year leasehold rights to Port Arthur, including the naval base and the peninsula around it, and ceded the southern half of Sakhalin Island, part of the Chinese territory lost to Russia in the treaty of Aihui in 1858, to Japan.

The battlefields happened entirely in Manchuria. The war brutally damaged China, as the battlefields of a large-scale warfare for one year and half. The war destroyed cities and villages alike, leveled the plantations. Refuges, over hundred thousands, were everywhere. An estimated 20,000 innocent civilian died. The financial loss, amounted to over 69 million tales worth of silver, was staggering. Nowhere China could ask for compensation. In addition, all the rights in Manchuria that China redeemed back from Japan by paying thirty million taels of silver went right back to Japan again. Russia lost the war, but she did not have to pay any war compensation, did not have to concede any territory. Everything Japan gained from Russia belonged to China. Japan, who had tasted the fruit of success, wanted more. From that moment on, Japan went on an aggressive expansion, initially to China, later to southeast Asia, and eventually she met with total destruction forty years later.

Russia's defeat was met with shock both in the West and across the Far East. Russia lost virtually its entire Pacific and Baltic Fleets, two of her three fleets. Russia could no longer sustain herself as a major power anymore. The embarrassing string of defeats inflamed the Russian people's dissatisfaction with their inefficient and corrupt Tsarist government, and resulted in the eventual downfall of Tsar's rule twelve years later.

On the other hand, Japan's prestige rose greatly as the Western Powers now regarded Japan as one of their equals and a modern nation. Japanese military gained the feeling of invincibility and began its efforts to dominate China and the rest of Asia. Such an ambition ended only forty years later by their defect at the end of World War II. The victories also transformed the balance of power in East Asia, resulting in a reassessment of Japan's recent entry onto the world stage.

When Japan replaced Russia in Manchuria after the Russo-Japanese War, the Japanese and U.S. governments pledged to maintain a policy of equality in Manchuria. The United States would recognize Japan's special interests in China by the Lansing Ishii Agreement. The Open Door Policy became ineffective by a series of secret treaties between Japan and the Western Powers, which promised Japan the German possessions in China, such as Qingdao, after German lost the World War I.

The Last Days of An Empire

Chapter 6

Self Protection Movement

During the Eight-Nation Alliance invasion, while the war was raging in the north, foreign warships and troops were also gathering in Shanghai area of Central China and Guangdong area of Southern China. The news of rampage from north arrived in the south every day. The animosity between Chinese and foreigners abounded. Any small incident could trigger a full-scale clash. The elites and business people were clearly worried.

Sheng Xuan Huai, the Nanyang Minister of Commerce and Zhang Jian, then a prominent industrialist, jointly proposed a plan for "Self Protection in the East and South." They sought endorsement from the Viceroys of Guangdong and Guangxi, Li Hong Zhang; of Hunan and Hupei, Zhang Zhi Dong; of Zhejiang and Jiangsu, Liu Kun Yi; and of Shandong, Yuan Shi Kai. The areas under their administration almost encompassed half China. The proposal was to ask these Viceroys to guarantee the safety of foreigners in these provinces in exchange of non-aggression. They conceived this plan to ask Viceroys' support because all these four Viceroys had openly criticized the Boxers.

On one side, they convinced the Viceroys; on the other side, they worked with the foreign consuls, who knew them well through the business deals. Soon both sides reached an agreement. Due to their effort, the scope of the Eight-Nation Alliance invasion did not spread into other provinces besides Zhili. The rest of the country was the business as usual.

Before Qing Court declared war against the Alliance, these Viceroys in the central and southern China and Sheng Xuan Huai met to discuss the strategy to prepare for the worst. They considered the Boxers coerced the

Qing Court to be against the foreigners, they did not want to take the side of an evildoer. As the events in the Zhili were unfolding, they also needed an emergency plan for the downfall of Qing Dynasty.

When Sheng Xuan Huai and Zhang Jian met the Viceroys, they reached the consensus quickly. The consensus was to avoid a foreign invasion in south and central China. To prepare for the worst, if Qing Court would collapse completely, they proposed that Li Hong Zhang would act as the president of China to avoid the country to become leaderless. All the Viceroys would back up Li to negotiate with the foreign powers. Both the government and the industrialists were in accord to the plan. Soon, they contacted foreigners and reached an understanding before the Alliance occupied Beijing.

During CiXi's exile in Xian, the Qing Court could not effectively carry out its administration orders. China was in the state of anarchy. The local governments were by themselves. The Viceroys of the province had the military as well s the administrative power. When the revolution came ten years later, many provinces declared independence. The Self Protection consensus sowed the seeds of fragmented China for the next fifty years. However, this is nothing new in Chinese history. During the transition of dynasties, sometimes, it took a long time for a new leader to emerge to unify the country. In the most recent history, China did not achieve the unification until Mao Ze Dong founded the Communist Regime in 1949, almost fifty years later.

The booming commercial and economic activities affected the regional governments in the central and southern China. Although the influence was slow and gradual, or sometimes unperceivable, however, it was irreversible and deeply rooted. It had a remote and profound impact in the formation of Chinese's industry later. They started to develop their own reform system, however regionally. The foundation they built would serve to speed up the industrial development in China later. As the old Chinese proverb says, "It takes ten years to plant a tree, but it takes one hundred years to create human resources."

When the Viceroys reached the agreement of the Self Protection Movement, they saw that northern China was raging the war against foreigners, and ten thousands of Chinese civilians were slaughtered, the Capital fell to foreign hands, and they still had to deal with the arrogant foreigners as if nothing had happened. Their hearts ached. However, in their minds, it was for the best of the country – the stability and construction.

Ironically, after the Self-Protection was in effect, with the recognition of the Western Powers, the business in the central and southern China thrived despite the chaotic situation in the north. On the contrary, the disturbance in the north severely impacted the imports of textile materials. It created a sudden shortage of textile.

Zhang Jian's textile factories went into full production and prospered. For years, Zhang Jian's textile business competing with the cheap imports got much needed relief. The profit soared. Between 1901 and 1907, Zhang Jian established nineteen large and small businesses. Zhang's business became the largest conglomerate in China. However, his business was not the only one.

Zhang Jian, the Founder of Chinese Conglomerate

Zhang Jian, like millions of Chinese youths pursuing a political career, studied Chinese literatures to take the Literature Exam, as Yuan Shi Kai did.

Zhang grew up in a family with the tradition of education. His father had a school. Therefore, since four years old, his father had best teachers in his school to instruct Zhang the Chinese Literatures, starting with the Sanzijin – the Three Letter Classics, a thirteenth century reading primer consisting of Confucian tenets in line of three characters. This was the first book read by millions of Chinese since the thirteenth century. It started with "When a man was born, he has good nature. Man's nature is similar but what they learned set them apart..."

More impressively, when he was five years old, he could recite from memory the "Thousand Character Classic" – a sixth century poem, another traditional reading primer.

Zhang was far more successful than Yuan in the Literature Exam system. In 1869, he passed the provincial level of the Literature Exam and received a title of Xiucai, equivalent of a bachelor degree.

In 1876, he went to work for General Wu Zhang Qing, the same general who later Yuan went to work for in 1881. He was General Wu's staff and performed as Wu's executive secretary. Later, they became two of the most trusted aides of General Wu. Yuan respected him as a professor.

During the Korean revolt in 1882, Qing Court transferred General Wu to Korea. Zhang went along. During his stay in Korean, he wrote most of the communication memorials and official reports for Wu to the Qing Court. He also wrote several detail memoranda to analyze the political and military situation in Korea and propose how to deal with the aftermath. Qing Court officials, such as Weng Tong He, GuangXu's private tutor, also an official, received Zhang's reports with favorable impression.

In 1884, he returned to China together with General Wu, while Yuan continued to station in Korea. Soon after, General Wu died. Zhang Jian left the Huai Army.

In 1885, he passed the National Literature Exam, and received the title of Juren, equivalent of the master's degree. In 1894, in the Special Literature Exam held for the sixtieth birthday of CiXi, he again passed and became a Zhuangyuan, equivalent to a Ph.D, the highest title of the Literature Exam system. It was an honorable title. In ancient China, if someone received Zhuangyuan title, the whole village would celebrate for him. It showed how Zhang Jian was good in the Chinese literature.

With his title, he received an offer to work in the Hanlin Institute – the Royal institute. In the next few years, the Institute transferred him several times within the system of royal institutes. He rose to the equivalent position of managing director for managing several provincial institutes – such as Xuanqing Institute in Jiangxi, Yingzhou Institute in Chongming, Wenzheng Institute in Jiangning, and Jinggu Institute in Anqing.

Before the Jiawu Sino Japanese War, Weng Tong He, representing GuangXu's opinion, was in favor of the war, but Li Hong Zhang, representing CiXi's opinion, was against the war. Weng had read many of the petitions from Zhang Jian, sent to Emperor GuangXu from Korea. He liked Zhang Jian's point of view. Therefore, when Zhang Jian returned from Korea, he recruited Zhang Jian to participate in the strategic policymaking. However, shortly after, Zhang's father died. Zhang had to return to his hometown to take care of the funeral for his father.

When China lost the Sino Japanese War, and signed the Maguan Treaty, Zhang joined the "Strong Study Association" founded by Kang You Wei in Shanghai.

The Last Days of An Empire

The year of 1896 signaled a turning point in Zhang's career when the Viceroy Zhang Zhi Dong recruited him and a few others to set up Bureaus of Commerce in central China. The scope of the Bureau of Commerce was to formulate the industrial policies, to define the target industries for development, to raise the funds, and to found government sponsored private and public companies.

With government help, Zhang founded a textile manufacturing company in Nantong near his hometown, called Dasheng Textile. Both the government of Zhang Zhi Dong and the Nanyang ministry of Sheng Xuan Huai invested in the company.

In 1898, Dasheng Textile Company officially broke ground. The production followed in the year after. It was during the Self Protection Period; Dasheng Textile saw its first profit.

In 1901, with the help of Viceroy of Jiangsu, Liu Kun Yi, Zhang founded Tonghai Plantation Company, to convert the barren land into cotton plantation. As the business model was proven, Zhang quickly expanded into other businesses as well – a cotton oil refinery, a flour factory, a metal tooling company, all located in the Tangzha Industrial Park, near Tongzhou.

Tongzhou was a port north of Yangtze River between Shanghai and Nanjing. It is located strategically for the logistics from Shanghai to the interior of central China. Out of necessity for the shipment of merchandize, raw materials and equipment, Zhang set up a large port facility with power plant of its own. A network of roads was also built. It became the cradle of the Chinese nascent light industry.

In view of the difficulty in recruiting educated and experienced human resources for the expansion of his business, in 1902, he proposed to the Viceroy Liu to set up a Western style normal school. However, the plan was not accepted. Zhang was determined to work on it. He took the profit from his business and set up his own school in 1903. It was the first normal school in China. His slogan was "Saving the nation by developing industries and education." His strategy in saving China by industrialization and education did not have an immediate impact on China's weakness and corruptness. However, the raised the long term strength for China as a nation.

His expansion of the industry and education did not stop at the fall of Qing Dynasty in 1911.

Later, he founded a company to manufacture power generators; a shipping company to transport along the Yangtze River; a college called Fudan, which evolved into a university of the same name, one of the leading universities in China; another college called Hehai Engineering College, which evolved into Hehai University later, one of the best engineering universities in China; a navigation school, which evolved into the Shanghai Maritime University; an oceanology school, which later is known as the Shanghai Ocean University; Tongji Medical School, Later changed into Tongji University. The list continued.

Other than schools, he also founded various organizations, among them: In 1905, he founded the first museum in China – Nantong Museum. In 1915, he set up a weather forecast station, and many others, like public libraries.

He died in 1926 at the age of seventy-three. He was a multimillionaire during his life, but he donated most of his money to set up schools, industries, and other enterprises.

Zhang Jian was the most successful industrialist in the late Qing Dynasty, but he was not the only one. The family of Rong Xi Tai was another example. Rong's descendents even prospered during the communist regime, due to their support of the communists, and became the Red Capitalist, one of the top riches in China.

Sheng Xuan Huai, the Father of Industrial Revolution in China

While Zhang focused on light industries, Sheng Xuan Huai, the Nanyang Minster of Commerce, was devoting himself to the development of heavy and financial industries, such as steel, railroad, mining, and banking. These industries required strong backup of the government and large capitals. They were always monopolies. Sheng was the one who laid the foundation of the business model of heavy industries in China.

Sheng was born in 1844 in a prominent family. His father was a Qing official, a friend of Li Hong Zhang. When he was twenty-six years old, he went to work for Li. Soon, Li appreciated his capability and promoted him. Since then, Li had given Sheng important assignments that Sheng never failed.

In 1872, he suggested to Li to found a shipping company, Li agreed and assigned him for the job that he proposed. It was the first Chinese shipping company -the Zhao Shang Shipping Company. It would become the largest Chinese private company, and Sheng was the chairman. Since then, he became the core member of Li Hong Zhang's reform team.

Li Hong Zhang's reform was not a political reform, but an industrial and economic reform. It was called the "Yangwu Movement" – literally meaning the Westernization Movement. The movement advocated a new business model of the state sponsored the private or public businesses to build and strengthen the national industries. Sheng was the one who implemented the Westernization Movement.

Within the next thirty years, he had achieved numerous "First" in China – the first shipping company in 1872, the Zhao Shang Shipping Company; the first telegraph company, the Tianjin Telegraph Company; the first river navigation company in 1886; the first mining exploration company in 1880's; the first metallurgical and coal company in 1896, Hanyieping Iron and Coal Company; the first long distance railroad from Beijing to Wuhan over one thousand miles; the first bank, the China Commercial Bank; the first modern Chinese university, Beiyang University, Later, changed the name into Tianjin University; China Red Cross; Shanghai Library; and Nanyang University in 1986, Later called the Jiaotong University; one of the best universities in China. He also sponsored several textile companies in Shanghai.

Even though GuangXu's "Hundred Days Reform" was a failure, however, not everything was in vain. The founding of Beiyang University was based on GuangXu's edict issued during the reform.

Sheng had the habit of collecting documents. He collected all his correspondences, writings, and journals. They are all preserved in Shanghai Library.

Sheng was also a philanthropist, especially in disaster relief. Since as early as 1877, when Li Hong Zhang sent him to relief the drought in northern China, he was deeply involved in the relief work, both using the government money and his person wealth. The founding of Chinese Red Cross organization in 1904 was his recognition of the Red Cross organization in the disaster relief. Through Red Cross, he also raised funds from the rich people in China. The Red Cross elaborated extensively to relief the refugees caused by the Russo-Japanese War in 1904. Sheng was one of the richest men in China. When he died in 1916, he left a will to donate half of his assets to charity. The day of his funeral procession, the streets in Shanghai where the procession went through were totally jammed. Ordinary citizens paid him respect for the last time.

These people followed the trend and promoted the industry and the business. Along the way, not only they prospered but also helped to lay the foundation of the modern industry in China.

"The Self Protection of East and South" signified the weakening of the power from the central government. Its authority could no longer reach many places in China anymore. It sowed the seed of a fragmented China for the next fifty years. It also showed people that Qing Court did not matter anymore. To the rest of the country, the Eight-Nation Alliance invasion was viewed as a local event in the north. CiXi's exile for one year effectively created anarchy.

On the positive side, the success of the "Self Protection" was entirely initiated by businessmen, who had the wisdom and courage to make a difference. It also highly elevated the social status and power of the business community, created a favorable environment by attracting talents to foster the Chinese nascent industry. It eventually provided a fertile ground for the rapid expansion of Chinese industries one hundred years later.

CiXi's Reform

By October 26, 1900, after more than two months on the road, CiXi arrived in Xian. Xian was the ancient capital of China from the time of Qin, the First Emperor of China, until the end of Tang Dynasty at the beginning of tenth century. It is the city, which had been the capital of China for over thousand years, most notably dynasties Qin, Han, and Tang. The mausoleum of Qin Shi Huang, the First Emperor of China, with its famous Terracotta Army is located 25 miles outside of Xian.

CiXi's temporarily residence in Xian was nowhere as comfortable as the Forbidden City, she was anxiously waiting for the result of negotiation, so that she could go back to Beijing.

When CiXi was in exile, she took the heir apparent Fu Hui with her. During the trip, CiXi had a chance to observe Fu Hui closely. Not only Fu Hui was dumb, he was also ill tempered and brusque. He was rude to GuangXu and called him "Foreign Devil's disciple" because GuangXu liked to learn English.

CiXi was quite upset and thought he was a way out of line. CiXi also realized that she was taken advantage by Fu Hui's father – Prince Duan. Without Price Duan's agitation, situation would not be this desperate. The foreigners were demanding the punishment of the responsible persons for the Boxers Rebellion. Nevertheless, the decision of using the Boxers was her own. She could not openly complain about it. However, CiXi wanted to distance herself from these gangs. On December 11, 1900, CiXi issued an edict to abolish the heir apparent title. This put to an end to the episode.

CiXi learned two lessons from this disastrous event. First, GuangXu's name still commanded respect domestically and overseas. Any attempt to downgrade GuangXu would only cause more protest. Second, the reform was a trend that no one could reverse. If CiXi would not go with the trend, she would be drowning in the historical current. This was not something she could fight. She realized that she would have to go along or better to take advantage of the trend.

On January 30, 1901, CiXi issued an edict in the name of GuangXu. The edict defended CiXi's position to crack down the "Hundred Days Reform," because it was chaotic and undermining the old systems without consideration of the viability of the new systems. It also explained that CiXi was not anti-reform, and was supporting GuangXu's effort on reform all along. CiXi would continue to support GuangXu to reform but on a different path. Now the government was soliciting officers, scholars and all walks of life to submit proposal of reform to study, whether on economics, education, political, industrial or business.

The edict received lukewarm reception, because CiXi did not quite have the creditability of reform. People took the edict as CiXi's excuse to pacify the nation, she really did not mean to reform. Meanwhile, the priority of the day was the negotiation with the Eight-Nation Alliance. Without concluding the negotiation, it was hard to talk about reform.

Without receiving much feedback, CiXi issued a second edict on February 13, 1901 also in the name of GuangXu. Again, there was no response. Finally, on April 21, CiXi decreed to set up a Reform Department, appointing Prince Qingqing, Li Hong Zhang, Yong Lu, Kun Gang, Wang Wen Shao and Lu Chuang Ling, all the heavy weight officers in the Qing Court. With those staffs on board, the credibility of reform augmented.

After the defeat of the Eight-Nation Alliance War, many Chinese were doing soul searching to find the root cause of the defeat. All kinds of viewpoints came with it. In addition, there was endless number of prescribed remedies for fixing the weakness of China. However, such a complex subject required more than an ordinary prescription.

The Viceroy of Jiangsu and Jiangxi, Liu Kun Yi, and Viceroy of Hunan and Hupei, Zhang Zhi Dong, both submitted proposals for reform. These proposals became the backbone of CiXi's reform plan. Qing Court quickly accepted the proposals.

In the next five years, Qing Court issued decrees for more than twenty-five reform policies. They embraced political, military, education, and legal reforms. The government also encouraged and helped to send students to study abroad. A comprehensive corporate law emulated after Western laws was also established. A foreign affair department was set up to deal with the diplomatic matters. Nation-wide Police department was established to maintain the law and order. Western style military schools were built to train officers in the newly organized army. The Imperial Literature Exam system for government service was eliminated; as a result, the Chinese classical system and its teaching material were replaced with a Western school system and teaching materials.

It is true that the reform did not save Qing Dynasty; nevertheless, it did contribute to the modernization of China. However, the reform also drew many criticisms. Many people viewed the reform nothing but decoration to mask the crackdown of Hundred Days Reform, and to appease the critics. It was a reform of palliative, would not strengthen the nation fundamentally. The corrupted core was still intact. China was still hopeless.

It remained true until July 1905, when Yuan proposed to change the core -the political system. The proposal aimed to change China fundamentally from the dynastic imperial system to the constitutional monarchy system. The whole nation cheered.

Grand Assessment Tour

The high-level officials dispatched to have a Grand Assessment Tour to the West to understand the secret of Western Powers to be powerful and rich eventually departed in October 1905.

They literally traveled around the world for almost one year. They went eastward, to Japan first, then the United States, Europe and Russia. Most heads of the states, including Emperor Meiji of Japan, President of the United States Theodore Roosevelt, and Russian Prime Minister Count

Sergei Yulyevich Witte received them. They visited congresses, libraries, parks, zoos, museums, factories, universities and many other places. It was an eye-opening trip for them. Everything was new and unimaginable. They saw parks and zoos for the first time, because there were no such things in China. Even simple things, such as Western toilet, were novelties. Everything appeared to be well organized in contrast to the chaotic manner in China. Everything also appeared to be clean, unlike the dirt filled, filthy streets in China.

The five officials were amazed at all: animals in the zoo, operas, beer halls, restaurants, food, streetcars, and the way people greeted each other by handshake. The grand library buildings with marble stairs leading to the second floor were like palace to them. The richness of the Western world was beyond their imagination.

On August 6, 1906, they returned to Tianjin. Yuan Shi Kai prepared a grand reception party for them. Yuan went to the train station to receive them, completed with honor guards and military band, playing Western military music reverberating through the train station.

Figure 18 The Chinese delegates of the Grand Assessment Tour in Rome

At the dinner party, Yuan asked, "You have traveled for so long. When Empress CiXi asks you about your opinions, how are you going to report your finding in this grand tour?"

All five of them caught by surprise and looked at each other waiting for the others to answer first. They had not had a chance to prepare their memorials yet. Yuan realized that for these officials to see and to hear about the Western world were one thing, but to come up with a workable political system was something all together different. The heads of the states who received them might have given them some ideas; however, as they did not understand the situation in China, there was no way for them to suggest anything useful.

After much thought, the Secretary of Interior, Dai Hong Ci, saying while pondering, "I think for us to catch up the West, we have to change into Constitution Monarchy system…"

Other officials echoed, followed by opinions one after another. Yet, there was still no concrete proposal, only personal opinions. After them finished their comments, Yuan said, "How long do you think this political reform will take?"

The officials started to mumble. One said, "Twenty years" Another one said, "Fifty years, maybe."

Yuan smiled: "But we do not have fifty years, or even twenty years. I think twelve years will be more desirable." Before others could intercept, he continued, "I have prepared a report as your reference material. You might use it where you see fit." He called his servant to bring the report to him.

Yuan showed the report to the officials. The report was very elaborated and thoughtful. Nothing in the report would offend or contradict Empress CiXi. The officials were delighted, thanked Yuan, "Mr. Yuan, you are very considerate. Thank you."

Yuan said modestly, "You are the one who toiled, you deserved the credit." In one stroke, Yuan's idea immediately became the idea of these five officials. Yuan was one-step closer to his goal.

Yuan's report detailed the steps to prepare for the constitutional monarchy. During the preparation phase, all the government organs would have to be set up to meet the requirement of constitutional monarchy. It was consistent with his earlier report that he submitted one year ago, which triggered the overseas trip for these officials. However, he worked out this report with great care and nicety of details. Yuan himself considered his report as a stroke of genius. He had asked Zhang Jian to work on the report for more than one year. He considered this plan much more far-sighted than GuangXu and Kang You Wei's reform plan, although many of the reform items were essentially the same.

However, from his point view, what would make the compelling difference was the procedure for implementation. He reasoned that one could not change something drastically without first preparing himself. He had done detail analysis of the failure of the Hundred Days Reform, excluding the factor of CiXi. He realized that many of GuangXu's new policies met a lot of resistance. If Yuan wanted to be successful, the resistance had to be avoided. Yuan had many years of hands-on experience in government administration. Especially, as the Viceroy of Zhili, he had already tried some of his policies in Zhili, without much resistance. He also realized that to educate the people was the key ingredient of the change. He had reasonable confident that the successful experiments he had done in Zhili could be repeated throughout the nation.

Yuan was a superb administrator; however, he was also overly ambitious. Sometimes, his ambition would overshadow his rational, putting his personal interest above all, and therefore made improper decisions, which provoked curses. In this report, he outlined the first phase plan for the constitutional monarchy was to re-organize government offices, without fundamentally asking Qing Court to share power with the Congress, which would not be set up until the end of twelve-year period.

However, before the five officials departed, they commented that they also had some ideas that they wanted to add. Yuan realized that their interest had to be preserved in the new reform plan, he laughed: "Of course, after all, this is your report!"

Audience

Few days later when they returned to Beijing, they had an audience with Empress CiXi and the Viceroy of Hunan Duan Fang presented a memorial to CiXi. The memorial suggested modeling the constitution after Japan and other reform policies such as military, agriculture, industry and commerce to take the best out of Japan and Germany. He also suggested using talents Han and Manchu alike without any bias. Furthermore, he suggested abolishing the system of eunuch. Dai Hong Ci also presented a memorial entitled "The Essence of Western Politics" saying, "Each country has its own political system. The United States is a federal government, while Britain and Germany are constitutional monarchy. Their political systems have a long history and are the essential ingredient of their success. It does not matter what kind of government system. They have one thing in common. That is, the respect of civil rights."

Five of them submitted their memorials to CiXi in turn. However, as Yuan expected, after they finished the presentation, CiXi was disappointed that the memorials were mere opinions without content. CiXi then asked, "Now, what do we do?"

Dai Hong Ci said, "We need to set up a constitution..."

CiXi was displeased, "Of course, I know we need a constitution. What do you think that I sent you overseas? However, do you have any idea how to prepare this constitution?"

At this point, Dai Hong Ci submitted Yuan's report. After reading Yuan's report, CiXi was delighted, "This is exactly what I wanted. She asked Yuan also join the committee to draft the constitution."

The Last Struggle

On August 26, 1906, CiXi called Yuan to Beijing for the first meeting in the draft of constitution together with the Grand Council. Five days later, on September 1, Qing Court announced its intention to draft a constitution. The essence of the edict was extracted from Yuan's original report.

This edict was received by the public with a big welcome. After all, China was going to have a constitution. This was the first time in China. Soon, the academic communities started to hold discussion meetings, seminars to celebrate Qing Court's announcement and to brainstorm the constitution. Business and news media communities followed the enthusiasm soon after. Tianjin, where Yuan resided and governed, had the biggest celebration. Many public offices hanged lanterns and decorated like a festival. Even the Chinese students in Japan were celebrating despite the fact that Japan was the base camp of Dr. Sun Yat Sen's revolution.

Zhang Jian had translated a copy of the Japanese Constitution three years ago. It had generated no interest. Now, suddenly, it became the best seller. Even the foreign media was also optimistic, "Finally, the tide of reform is really coming to China. This time, China will make it."

On the second day of the edict, Qing Court formed a Political System Reform Committee to define the new government organization. It included the five officials who went overseas, Yuan, members of Grand Council and representatives from the provincial government. This was the first time in Qing history or Chinese history that a political reform was formally launched. Due to the sensitive subjects discussed, the meetings were held clandestinely.

However, people were naturally very sensitive to any reorganization. Rumors were abounding. Everybody with a vested interest in the existing political system was trying to find whether the reform would impact his position, his future, therefore his fortune.

The Last Days of An Empire

As soon as the representatives from provinces arrived in Beijing, they were confined in a closed quarter in the Forbidden City to have intensive meeting on the agenda of reform. The subject of matter discussed in the meeting was sensitive and treated as highly confidential.

The background of the committee members was diverse. Some were from the old bureaucratic system; others were from the newly promoted officials who had studied abroad. For those who received Western education, some studied in Japan, others from Europe and the United States. The discussion of the governmental organization became a fight for turf. Each of the committee member represented interest groups behind them. The proposal had a difficult birth.

The meeting went on for days. Because Yuan's proposal was the baseline for discussion, it served as a baseline for discussion. It called for the elimination of Grand Council and formation of a cabinet as the first step of the constitutional monarchy system. The Grand Council reported to the emperor or the empress, but the new cabinet would report to the prime minister, rather than the emperor. In turn, the congress, not the emperor, would elect the prime minister. The formation of the congress would take longer. However, before the congress was formed, Empress CiXi would appoint a prime minister.

At lower level, many branches of the government, which had been in place for thousands of years, such as Li Ministry – responsible for all the educational affair, including the Imperial Literature Exam; Hanlin Institute – the royal academy; House of Discipline and Audit – the institute responsible for the discipline of royal families and court officials. Other branches were created, combined or changed names – such as the formation of Court of Auditors, Department of Transport, and Advisory Council. All the military organizations were nationalized under the Department of Military, which consisted of the Department of Army and Department of Navy.

The change was so dramatic, that it was even more momentous than the failed Hundred Days Reform. The turn of direction in the discussion also surprised Yuan because he did not expect his framework would create such controversy. Any new suggest from committee member was motivated by someone ' s self-interest and others would immediately scrutinize its implication to them and distort the original suggestion beyond recognition. Along the discussion, some cheered, some were lost in the thoughts and others were worried and visibly upset.

The second part of the proposal was to select the candidates for each new branches of the government. Most conflict arose this part. The son of Prince Qingqing, Zai Zhen proposed Prince Qingqing to be the Prime Minister of the Cabinet and Yuan the Deputy Prime Minister. Yuan had privately endorsed it in exchange of Zai Zhen being the Minister of the Industry, Commerce and Agriculture, which was probably the most lucrative position. In fact, Yuan had long discussed to Prince Qingqing and Zai Zeng about this arrangement. When Prince Qingqing had doubted whether his son was up to this job, Yuan said, "Don't worry. Even GuangXu could be emperor at four years old, why Zai Zeng cannot be the minister." Under Yuan's recommendation, Zai Zeng went to Japan to have a tour of the Japanese industry, and came back as an expert in the area.

Grand Council was the highest executive office in Qing Court. It reported directly to the Emperor, in the final days of Qing, to Empress Dowager CiXi. There were six Grand Council members. Yuan was not one of them. In the proposed Cabinet, there were only three deputy prime ministers, including Yuan. That meant that three members of Grand Council would lose their prominent jobs. Strong reactions from them were expected.

Qu Hong Ji, as a member of Grand Council, was also a member of the committee. He knew exactly Yuan's ambition and ploy. He was even more convinced by the active role Yuan played in the meetings. He was determined to undermine it.

Much other discussion followed. The Department of Officials, which acted as the human resources department for all levels of government personnel assignment, was to be eliminated. It was the first one to protest strongly to CiXi. The Department of Discipline Inspection sent a petition to CiXi saying that only those who were afraid of inquiry would propose to remove the department.

Qu knew many people who would be severely affected by this proposal, and he secretly passed the information to these people. Qu also told them confidentially that he would support them in front of CiXi if they would submit petitions. As Qu secretively instigated the opposition, the opposition gained momentum. Qu gradually gained an upper hand in front of CiXi. He reported to CiXi that Yuan was trying to put all his cronies into the high-level positions. To him, this meeting was Yuan's plan to share the booty. Qu was not against the reform, but was to destroy Yuan and his ambition.

Numerous petitions arrived in CiXi every day. Unknowing that Qu was behind these oppositions, CiXi sought Qu's opinions on these petitions. One of the reasons that Qu gained the high trust from CiXi was that he was incorruptible. Qu had a reputation that he never received any bribe nor he could be induced by anyone. To CiXi, his suggestions were always unbiased. Taking this advantage, Qu sided with many of the petitioners to defend their course.

The reaction to the reform was not unlike the resistance against GuangXu's Hundred Days Reform. However, this time, both sides were trying to bias CiXi, and without knowing Qu's ruse, Yuan was count on CiXi support.

Meanwhile, the fact that Yuan would become the Deputy Prime Minister also upset CiXi. She learned that Yuan supported Zai Zeng to be the Minister of Industry, Commerce and Agriculture. She knew that Zai Zeng was extremely incapable. She knew that Prince Qingqing was close to Yuan. She suspected that it was an exchange of favors. She had intended to appoint Shang Xuan Huai for the Minister of Industry, Commerce and Agriculture position. Sheng was one of Li Hong Zhang's most trusted men, and she knew that Sheng had contributed in building many industries in the past.

A combination of factors gradually swayed CiXi that Yuan was not the right man to lead this reform. Yuan's ambition was exposed through many of the personnel selections for the new branches of the government. CiXi did not want to see Yuan gained much more power. She knew that Yuan was a capable administrator, but she also realized that Yuan was overly ambitious. Yuan was not the second Li Hong Zhang that CiXi thought he was. CiXi wanted to use Qu to counterbalance Yuan. CiXi tried to distance herself from Yuan. She also asked Qu to monitor the progress of drafting the proposal.

As sensitive as Yuan, he quickly realized CiXi's attitude toward him changed. He was debating what position he should take. One day, when CiXi summoned him, "Many people complained about your reform, what you are going to do about it?" She threw petitions to Yuan.

Yuan was already sweating with fear. However, he made his final strike, "Your Highness, the reform is critical for the survival of Qing Dynasty. The old, feudal and corrupted force must be eliminated to pave the way for the reform. Qing had tried the reform many times, if we fail this time, we would lose all the credibility to the people. It would be impossible to do reform in the future. Therefore, I ask Your Highness to stand firm on the reform and kill a few who dare to resist, then the plan can move forward smoothly."

CiXi was not moved. She scorned, "Yuan Shi Kai, you are holding the military power. Why don't you around them up and kill them all?"

Yuan was now fully scared, he kneeled down and ask for forgiveness, while Qu was watching on the side. Yuan said, "How dare I do this? I request Your Highness to take back all my military duties."

CiXi did not say anything, just sent him away. As Qu correctly figured, CiXi would not tolerate anyone trying to gain advantage out of her. Yuan might have had chance to push through the reform if he were not so self-interested.

On the same day, Yuan resigned from the member of the reform committee. Soon, CiXi assigned Qu to finish the draft of the proposal for reform.

Under Qu, the scope of the reform was greatly scaled down. The Grand Council was intact. The plan of formation of the Cabinet and the position of prime minister was abolished. However, six members of Grand Council were reduced to two – only Prince Qingqing and Qu Hong Ji stayed. Most of the government branches stayed. Some changed the names to appease the public opinion. For example, the Ministry of National Budget changed its name as the Department of Treasury. Some new branches, whose functions did not exist before, such as the Department of the Telegraph and Post Office, were created.

All the Armies and Navies, including the Beiyang Army, were transferred under the jurisdiction of newly created Department of Defense. The military force was nationalized. After this reshuffle, Manchu people occupied most of the key positions in the government. Very few Han officials remained.

The reform also had a positive side. Qing Court committed a timetable: In 1908, Qing Court would publish the draft of the Constitution, and in 1915, Qing Court would convene the first congress meeting.

When the Qing Court officially issued an edict for the cabinet organization of the reform plan, Yuan's confidant Zhang Yi Ling commented to Yang, "In this reform, Han people lost big time. Manchu controlled all the key positions."

Yuan sighed, "I am afraid Qing's end is near!"

Yuan returned to Tianjin. He would not go to Beijing again. He became reclusive, and inactive. His enthusiasm in the past was all vanished. One day, when his friend, the disposed member of Grand Council Xu Shi Zhang came to see him, and told me that he heard in the Court, "Those Manchus were commenting that you still hold powerful army. I think their prejudice against you is strong."

Yuan said dismally, "If this is what they worried, I have no choice." Immediately, he wrote a memorial to the Qing Court, claiming that since all the military forces were nationalized, he had no reason to hold on to Beiyang Army. He wanted to resign from the post as commander of the Beiyang Army, and hand over the army to the Secretary of Defense, Tieliang.

After he submitted the memorial, he was still secretly hoping that CiXi would give consideration of his past contribution and asked him to stay. However, after several days that he waited without receiving the reply. He was becoming desperate. He submitted another memorial to give up all this posts in control of the railroad, telegraph, and navigation industries that he had created in the past.

On November 20, 1906, he received the reply from the court, that his wishes were all granted. For more than two years that he had worked on this reform plan, he did not expect that the result would be like this. He became nobody in the Qing Court.

However, Qu knew that even Yuan was defeated; he was not completely out of the picture. With Yuan's deep-rooted connections, and the loyal support of many generals in the Beiyang Army, it was quite possible that Yuan might counter attack one day, if CiXi changed her mind. He needed to deliver a final blow and finish with Yuan once for all. He was trying to identify a way to achieve this. Finally, he settled on Cen Chun Xuan.

Cen Chun Xuan

Cen was Yuan's rival. In late Qing, a popular saying went that "There is Yuan in the north and Cen in the south." Both built up their reputation through their military careers. They were not only rivals but also dead enemies.

Cen was a descent of Miao minority in the southern of China, and born into a prominent family. His father served as the Viceroy of Yunnan and Guizhou, two provinces neighboring with Burma, and Fujian and Taiwan during his career. His father built a reputation to lead the successful campaign to suppress the Miao uprising, and fought the French in Vietnam.

At the age of twenty-four, the Cen Jr. passed the Imperial Literature Exam. He was offered a Court position. Soon he became a judge in the equivalent of superior court in Qing Court. In the subsequent years, he followed his father in his campaigns and built a reputation of successful military leader of his own.

During the Hundred Days Reform, he was quite close with Kang's reformers. He even submitted memorial to Emperor GuangXu to express his view that all the government branches were over staffed, and should be made leaner. GuangXu appreciated his suggestion and dispatched him to be the commissioner to work with the Viceroy of Guangdong and Guangxi. However, Cen did not get along with the then Viceroy Tang Zhong Ling, and was asked to be transferred. His request was granted and was transferred to Gansu – a province at the northwest of China with large population of Muslim.

During CiXi's trip of exile, he led a troop to meet CiXi half way to escort. CiXi was impressed.

When CiXi arrived in Xian, she promoted Cen to be the Viceroy of Shanxi, where he built a Shanxi Western School with the help of British missionary Timothy Richard, an influential missionary who dedicated himself to serve China and made an impact on the Chinese revolution and Christianity. Later, the school developed into the Shanxi University.

Cen considered education as the top priority in modernizing China. He built more than ten higher education institutes. Besides the Shanxi Western School, there were also Sichun High Level School, Guangdong Military Academy, Guangdong and Guangxi Department of Education, Military High School, Political and Law School, Guangdong and Guangxi Industrial and Business School, School of Forest Resources, Women Normal School, School of Sericulture, and many others. In all the provinces that he had served as Viceroy, he had laid down the foundation for modern education.

Cen gained a reputation of a tough administrator, who was merciless in purging the corrupted officials. He relentlessly and ruthlessly uncovered large-scale corruptions, and requested the extradition of several high level officials who fled to Europe after prosecution. The foreigners called him the "Manchu Tiger." By doing so, he had offended quite a few powerful people in Beijing, who had connections with those that Cen prosecuted. Prince

Qingqing was one of them. However, Cen was not afraid because he could count on CiXi's support.

For his merciless prosecution of the corrupted officials, he earned a title of "the Butcher of Officials," together with the other two "Butchers" – Yuan Shi Kai and Zhang Zhi Dong.

Yuan gained his nickname as the "Butcher of People," when he cruelly killed many Boxers in Shandong. While Zhang Zhi Dong gained his title of the "Butcher of Money," because he was a big spender in his pet projects for modernization.

In 1903, Cen petitioned Qing Court for the constitution reform, and supported Zhang Jian to organize an association called "Society for the Preparation of Constitution." He was one of the strong advocates of constitution reform.

In 1906, when Cen was the Viceroy of Guangdong and Guangxi, Prince Qingqing persuaded CiXi to transfer Cen to be the Viceroy of Yunnan and Guizhou to suppress an uprising. Cen considered this as a demotion, since the Viceroy of Guangdong and Guangxi, two of the most important and rich provinces in the south, were a much more prominent and strategic position than the Viceroy of two remote and poor provinces in the southwest. Cen claimed that he was sick and refused to take the job. Since then he developed strong enmity toward Prince Qingqing.

In April 1907, when he received a telegram from Qu Hong Ji to ask him to Beijing, he no longer pretended to be sick. He took a train to Beijing immediately. Upon arriving in Beijing, he went straight to Qu's home. The two found alliance bonded by their burning desire to defeat their enemies – Prince Qingqing and Yuan Shi Kai.

Qu and Cen pondered and discussed the strategy to sway CiXi. Once they agreed, Qu requested CiXi to summon Cen. When Cen met CiXi, he appeared to be moved by CiXi's kindness, since he had not seen CiXi for several years. He said that he was serving the country in the provinces, that he had many observations of the country's current situation, was saddened by it, and wanted to report to CiXi. He continued that the corruption was rampant and many officials held onto their power to benefit themselves, without the consideration for the country and the people. He cited one of the major cases of corruption of a crony of Prince Qingqing, Zhou Rong Yau. He also implied that Yuan relied on Prince Qingqing's influence to enhance and build up his power. He commanded Beiyang Army as if it were his army.

He mixed something CiXi had already known with something CiXi did not know in order to gain credibility of his story. He gradually imprinted an unfavorable impression of Prince Qingqing on CiXi's mind. However, it would take much longer to work on CiXi to get what he wanted. He needed to be close to CiXi. He found an excuse to ask CiXi to offer him a position in Beijing so that he could serve the country better. After reviewing some suitable newly created positions, CiXi appointed him as the Minister of Telegraph.

Cen's appointment created quite a disturbance in the capital, because his reputation as the "Butcher of Officers." People were speculating that CiXi wanted to use him to "clean up" the corruption in the capital. Prince Qingqing was particularly concerned. He had already got the cue from CiXi that Cen was implying his embezzlement. He could also feel that CiXi was no longer as friendly to him as before. He was wondering whether CiXi would take a next step on him. He went to see Yuan for some advice. Yuan heard the news and was worried himself. He knew that Qu sponsored Cen to Beijing. Qu had already totally defeated him in this reform; He was afraid that Qu would not stop there and continued to finish him off. Indeed, Cen soon took the next step. As they had expected, it did not take long for Cen to launch an attack.

Yuan's Fall

In the old Chinese system, which Qing inherited, in the Imperial Court, any official had the right to impeach any other officials. The emperor himself would be the judge. If the emperor was wise, the system actually worked quite well. There was the effect of vigilance among the high-level officials so that they would be more careful to abuse their power to be corrupt. However, if the emperor himself was incompetent, or could be easily swayed, it could be abused to frame the rivals.

One of the reform items in 1905 was to redefine the administration regions of China. To unify the administrative system, and strengthen the control, the entire special district in peripheral areas of China – Manchuria, Xinjiang, Tibet, and Mongolia changed into the same provincial system in China proper. Manchuria was redefined as three provinces – Fengtian, Jilin, and Heilungjiang. Yuan's ambition for long was to include Manchuria into

144

his Beiyang system. He was working to appoint his cronies in Beiyang to take the key positions in Manchuria. His approach was to achieve this through Prince Qingqing.

In November 1906, not long after the end of Russo-Japanese War, CiXi sent Prince Qingqing's son Zai Zeng, then the newly appointed Minister of Industry, Commerce and Agriculture, and Minister of Civil Service Administration, Xu Shi Chang, to inspect the devastated Manchuria. The purpose was to understand the Japanese penetration in Manchuria and prepare a recovery plan after the destructive war. After all, Manchu was the homeland of Manchu people that was most dear to their heart. They departed from Beijing on November 15 and returned on January 4, 1907.

On their way to Manchuria, they went to visit Yuan in Tianjin. At that time, Yuan had already been stripped most of his positions, and was quite depressed. Yuan held a welcome party for the two ministers. In the party, Yuan hired famous singer in Tianjin, Yang Cui Xi, to perform a show. Yang was strikingly pretty and gifted with a beautiful voice. At eighteen years old, she was already a celebrity. Her biggest supporter was a deputy director in the Tianjin Police Department – Tuan Zhi Gui, one of Yuan's cronies.

When Zai Zeng saw Yang and her show, he was enchanted by her right away. Zai praised Yang's beauty and performance without reservation. Nothing could hide from Yuan's observation. Immediately, he had a plan.

When Zai Zeng and Xu Shi Chang came back to Tianjin from the trip to Manchuria, Yuan again invited them to dinner, and asked them to stay in Tianjin for a couple of days. In the dinner party, Yuan asked Yang Cui Xi to join and introduced her to Zai Zeng.

Also in the dinner party, Yuan gave Zai Zeng a list of names, and asked him to deliver to Prince Qingqing, saying that he recommended these people to be the potential candidates of Viceroy and Deputy Viceroys in Manchuria. In addition, Yuan also asked Zai Zeng to take a bank note of a considerable sum to his father Prince Qingqing. However, Zai Zeng's attention was entirely devoted to Yang, and hastily agreeing everything that Yuan said. Yuan paid Yang Cui Xi handsomely to ask Yang to go with Zai Zeng as mistress. Zai took Yang home.

Three months later, with Prince Qingqing's arrangement, Yuan's wish came true: Xu Shi Chang became the Viceroy of East Three Provinces, the renamed Manchuria; Tang Shao Yi was the Deputy Viceroy of Fengtian;

Zhu Jia Bao was the Deputy Viceroy of Jilin, and Tuan Zhi Gui was the Deputy Viceroy of Heilongjiang.

Somehow, Cen got hold of all these facts, and submitted a memorial to impeach Prince Qingqing and Yuan. CiXi was very displeased, and asked Qu to draft an edict for the retrieval of the appointments. All Yuan's cronies for the positions of the East Three Provinces were removed. Zai Zeng also voluntarily resigned his Minister position. CiXi also commented in front of the only two Staffs of Grand Council left – Qu and Prince Qingqing that if Prince Qingqing did not give CiXi a satisfactory explanation, she would consider to replace him as the Chief Staff. This was the last heavy blow to Prince Qingqing.

Qu would not stop there. He further issued the edict for the detail investigation and prosecution. Prince Qingqing and Yuan were desperate. The persons that Qu assigned to investigate were all Yuan's enemies. In doing so, Qu could be sure that they would do their best job.

By the time that the investigators wanted to dig into detail, Zai Zeng, already under the urge of Yuan, sent Yang Cui Xi back to Tianjin and Yang denied that she ever served Zai Zeng. The bank note was also a dead-end. After all, both Prince Qingqing and Yuan were powerful enough to stop the track of their wrongdoing. The investigation went nowhere.

CiXi did not want to inflate this case anymore. The in fighting weakened Qing Court. The implicated people were all the pillar of Qing Court, and that CiXi had to rely on. During the past few decades, CiXi relied heavily on Rong Lu as the guardian of the Qing Court and the royal family, and on Li Hong Zhang as the administrator of the nation. Both were capable and royal to her. Rong Lu had protected her from the very first day she launched the coup against the powerful Sushun and grabbed the power. Without Rong Lu, she would have probably died then. Li Hong Zhang dedicated himself for her over thirty years, without complain, always shared her burden even to the last day of his life. When he was terminally ill, coughing with blood, he negotiated with the Eight-Nation Alliance for the Treaty. He had kept her in her position without letting foreigners to abolish her. She was truthfully grateful.

With Li Hong Zhang's passing in 1901 and Rong Lu's passing in 1903, CiXi was like losing two arms. There was nobody she could rely on as she depended on them. She promoted Prince Qingqing, her husband's brother to replace Rong Lu, hoping that Prince Qingqing would be another Rong Lu. She promoted Yuan Shi Kai to replace Li Hong Zhang, hoping that Yuan would be another Li Hong Zhang. However, they were so different. Prince Qingqing was greedy and corrupt. Yuan was ambitious and not reliable. Conversely, what else could she do?

She was at loss. Lately, she felt that her heath was deteriorating. The reform was not making progress as she wanted with too much resistance. How many years more she could hold onto power? What would happen if she died? She wanted to set up the constitutional monarchy before she died. She believed that it was the right way to extend Qing Dynasty's life. However, it was a long way. She was not sure that she would see it implemented.

The Japanese aggression in Manchuria was getting more openly. They already took the Manchuria by essence if not by name. They opened mines. They cut the forest. They harvest the crops. In addition, they used the Chinese labors to build railroads, highways. The Japanese garrisons were everywhere. In the Port Arthur, there were only Japanese warships, no more Chinese warships.

In the central and southern China, Westerners came and went as they wish. They built churches where they wished. They taxed the Chinese exports. They took a lion share of the Chinese import tax. They sold as much as opium as Chinese market would buy. CiXi wondered how everything was going to end. She felt so powerless and helpless. She wished that she had not used the money of Beiyang Fleet to build her garden. She could still imagine that Li was imploring her to give him funds for the navy. However, everything was too late.

Yes, she was unhappy about Prince Qingqing to gain personal benefits by assigning positions of Viceroy to Yuan's cronies. Nonetheless, CiXi was also grateful to Prince Qingqing that she exiled from Beijing during the Eight-Nation Invasion, most of her trusted court officials were nowhere to be seen. She was so grateful that Prince Qingqing came early to meet her and wanted to protect her. Finally, she decided to let Prince Qingqing to stay behind to maintain order in the Forbidden City and Beijing. She knew that it was a risky task because there was no telling what the invasion troop would do. She knew that during the invasion of Second Opium War, the court official who defended the Yuanmin Garden was killed in the combat. The situation in Beijing on the day of her exile from Eight-Nation Alliance invasion was chaotic. Killing and burning were going on in the city. However, Prince Qingqing was unafraid. He told CiXi that he would defended the Forbidden City to the end. As the Chief of Staff, Prince

Qingqing was the highest person in command in China besides CiXi and Emperor GuangXu. CiXi also knew that during the negotiation with the Eight-Nation Alliance, he and Li Hong Zhang were defending her position without compromise. She was forever grateful to Prince Qingqing. She wanted to punish Prince Qingqing for his wrongdoing, but to punish on her own terms. She did not want to be coerced into punishing him differently.

Yuan Struck Back

Few days later, on May 18, 1907, CiXi invited women of foreign dignities in Beijing and Tianjin to her Yihe Garden for a get together party for the first time. This was at the advice of her lady-in-waiting of Princess Der Ling. Princess Der Ling was the daughter of Yu Keng, a Manchu White Banner. Yu Keng had served as ambassador of Qing in Japan and France. Der Ling therefore was educated overseas. She also served as CiXi's translator. Due to her background, she was quite favorable to the foreigners. Through her, CiXi learned more about Westerners, their custom, their habit, their manners and their history. Being with Der Ling became one of CiXi's favorable distractions. Der Ling would tell CiXi her experience in Japan and in Europe, the places that she had visited, the interesting things that she had seen. As CiXi learned more, her xenophobia and bias against Westerns were abridged. Der Ling also told her to socialize with the women of foreign dignities to polish her image, and interview with Western reporters to write a favorable review about her. For the first time, CiXi decided to have a party for the foreign women and reporters.

Afternoon, the guests were starting to arrive in luxury carriages with the sedan chair, dressed in bright and attractive Western clothes – the styles featured form-fitting gowns with high waists, ankle-length skirts and long tunic-like jackets. The dresses were exquisite to CiXi, however, not unpleasant, even graceful and elegant. The women also used large, broad brimmed hats trimmed with masses of feathers and occasionally complete stuffed birds, or decorated with ribbons and artificial flowers. Their masses of wavy hair were fashionable, swept up to the top of the head and gathered into a knot.

In the party, the band played Western music; the garden was filled with chats and laughter, words with strange accents and unknown tones. Food and drinks were served. CiXi created a quite an impression on the foreigners.

The foreigners were surprised to find Empress CiXi was not like the media had portrayed of her at all – old, fierce, witch-like dictator, rather they found her to be kind, charming, dignified, warm and friendly. With Der Ling's translation, CiXi was free talk to the foreign women. The women also praised CiXi generously. CiXi felt relaxed after many days of stress.

The wife of the American Ambassador came to compliment CiXi. Amid the casual conversation, the American woman suddenly asked, "I heard that the Chief of Staff was removed!" CiXi was surprised by the comment because it had not been announced yet. CiXi was visibly upset. She asked Der Ling to ask the American where she got the information. She said that it was from Thames News.

After the party, CiXi immediately asked her trusted aide Li Lian Ying to produce the newspaper that the American woman mentioned. The newspaper confirmed her comment. Furthermore, the news in the Thames quoted a source from a Chinese newspaper called "The Capital News." The only person who had knowledge of what she said about replacing Prince Qingqing were Prince himself and Qu. Nobody else but Qu could have leaked the information to the media. CiXi suddenly felt that she was betrayed and developed distaste toward Qu.

When Yuan heard that CiXi was displeased about the news leak from his informants in the Forbidden City, he immediately searched for the same paper. When he found out that the chief editor of the "The Capital News" was Wang Kang Nian, he pounded on the desk: "Qu Hong Ji, I got you!"

He went to see Prince Qingqing the next day.

When Yuan visited him, Prince Qingqing was at his low mood. However, he saw Yuan was joyful. He was puzzled: "Do you have good news?"

Yuan said, "Yes, I have a good idea."

He continued with his plan. After he finished talking, Prince Qingqing was elated. Immediately, they worked out a plan of attack.

Qu did not realize that CiXi was already unhappy about him. He continued to push, however skillfully, when CiXi would make a decision to replace Prince Qingqing. CiXi was non-committal; nonetheless, she disliked Qu even more.

On May 27, a telegraph arrived from the Viceroy of Guangdong Zhou Fu, asking Qing Court to reinforce to suppress the uprising there. Without anybody knowing, Yuan was the one who arranged this urgent telegram. It was Yuan's plot.

In the Court audience the next day, nothing was unusual. CiXi showed the telegram to her staff and asked, "There is an urgent telegram from Guangdong asking for military reinforcement, what you think?" She explained the detail.

Qu quickly replied, "We should ask Zhou prepare himself and do his best."

Prince Qingqing followed, "Zhou Fu is asking for Court's support. Apparently, he cannot handle this by himself. I suggest we send someone to help him."

CiXi frowned, "Whom can we send?"

Prince Qingqing glanced at Qu and said, "To lead the army to fight rebels in Guangdong, I think Cen is the best candidate."

CiXi agreed that Cen was a good candidate. At the same time, she wanted to test Qu, since she suspected that Qu asked Cen to come to Beijing and two of them worked as alliance to fight Prince Qingqing and Yuan.

Without showing her intention, she asked Qu lightly, "Qu Hong Ji, what do you think?"

Not knowing it was a trap, Qu said, "Cen came to Beijing not long ago, and he is not healthy. I am afraid that he is not capable of leading a military campaign right now,"

Qu's reply confirmed CiXi's suspect. She did not say more to Qu but called Cen in. Shortly Cen arrived and greeted CiXi. He sensed a strange quietness among CiXi, Prince Qingqing and Qu. He knew that something wrong happened, but could not figure out what.

Before he had second thought, CiXi said to him, "Cen, since you came to Beijing, you have done a good job. I appreciated what you have done for this Court. However, there is an urgent request from Guangdong to put down an uprising. I think you are the best candidate. Once more, you can provide your best service for this Court. I want you to go."

Cen now realized that he was deliberately sent away. For whatever reason CiXi said, he felt that it was only an excuse. Others could do the job. From what he knew, the uprising in Guangdong was not a big issue. He wanted to say something but could not. He could only thank CiXi for the appointment and left.

Yuan had accomplished the first step of his plan – breaking the Qu and Cen alliance.

After Cen left, CiXi told Prince Qingqing and Qu, "With Cen taking charge of this assignment, I think the uprising can be pacified. Qu Hong Ji, please issue an edict soon." The subject was closed.

Once Qu and Cen were separated, Prince Qingqing and Yuan were ready to move onto the second step, to deliver a severe blow to Qu.

On the same day, Prince Qingqing went to see Li Lian Ying. Since Prince Qingqing's downfall, many selfish officials altered their attitude toward Prince. Prince felt deeply that without power he was nothing. It saddened him but it was a way of life.

Li Lian Ying was different. He knew better. He had seen the ups and downs of many court officials over the years. He would never write off someone only because he was down temporarily. He also realized that to treat someone well in his depressed mood was the best time to win him over. If one day, this person could rise again, he would appreciate Li. On the other hand, if this person was gone forever, Li had nothing to lose. A good manner did not cost him anything.

On that day, when he met with Prince Qingqing, he greeted Prince as pleasant as usual: "Good day, how is my Lord? What brought you here today?"

Prince brought him to a closed quarter and produced a bank note, and a package of documents. Prince first called Li's attention to the bank note. It was a considerable amount. Li knew that Prince needed his favor, and pretended: "My Lord, I cannot accept your money. If there is something that I can do, I will be most glad to be your service."

Prince insisted on giving him the bank note and said, "What I worried about is that the evidences seem to show that the Staff of Grand Council Qu Hong Ji is a sympathizer of Kang You Wei gang of rebels. I am afraid that the way CiXi trusted Qu; it may lead to undesirable consequences. I have collected some evidences for you so that you can show it to CiXi."

It was straightforward for Li Lian Ying. Earlier, CiXi had already asked him to search the newspapers on this subject. Li took a look of the information provided by Prince Qingqing. He drew a deep gasp.

What Yuan and Prince Qingqing compiled was not only the news of removal of Prince Qingqing as Staff of Grand Council, but also a collection of editorial articles in favor of the Hundred Days Reform and Kang's activities in Japan. Several articles advocated supporting the return of GuangXu. The newspaper was like a voice of Kang You Wei. It clearly showed the position of the Capital News. The second part of the information was even more staggering. It was a biography of the chief editor -Wang Kang Nian. He was indeed one of Qu Hong Ji's disciples. It showed that their relationship dated back to long time ago.

For what Li Lian Ying understood of CiXi, he knew exactly what CiXi would do. While Li was ally of either Prince Qingqing or Yuan, however, over the long period, Yuan had offered Li many paybacks. Prince Qingqing also treated Li cordially. On the other hand, Qu Hong Ji simply considered Li as a retainer, not deserving any more respect than a servant did. Li had no problem of seeing Qu's disgrace. He replied, "This is a small matter that I am glad to be your service."

Four days later, the package of information was laid on the desk of CiXi. Li Lian Ying said calmly, "On Your Highness order, I have collected more information about the Capital News."

CiXi would not imagine that this information was collected by Yuan. She thought Li was following her order to collect it. She could not envision that her most trusted official was a sympathizer of rebels. To her surprise, the Capital News editor Wang Kang Nian was Qu Hong Ji's disciple. Not only a simple disciple, the evidence also showed that their families were close. It was impossible for Qu not to know what was published in the Capital News.

Furthermore, several recent articles severely criticized Prince Qingqing, and strongly praised Qu and Cen. To CiXi, the newspaper was serving Qu and Cen. CiXi had the feeling that she was cheated. She had misplaced her trust on Qu. Even though Prince Qingqing was corrupt, but at least he was loyal. In addition, CiXi needed somebody loyal and reliable that she could count on. Fortunately, she had not done anything stupid to remove Prince Qingqing. Otherwise, Qu would be the only person in the Grand Council and would be uncontrollable.

CiXi waited for a few days. She did not want to make a hasty decision. She had other sources to reconfirm Wang Kang Nian's relationship with Qu. It was indeed, as Li Lian Ying's information had showed. She also remembered that Qu had petitioned the pardon of Kang three times.

She sighed. Qu had served her well since 1900, out of the recommenda-
tion of Li Hong Zhang. For seven years, Qu had done CiXi's assignments to
CiXi's full satisfaction. Qu was diligent, quick witted and easy to work.
Qing Court was already depleted with capable officials. Once Qu was gone,
Prince Qingqing would be the only one in Grand Council. She knew that
Prince was not competent in his job and would not be able to handle the
daily business for the country on his own. CiXi worried that who else could
do this job.

CiXi already felt old at seventy-two. She did not have the energy or the
patient to read the hundreds of daily court memorials coming from four
corners of the nation. CiXi entrusted Qu to review many court memorials
and to make appropriate decisions based on the analysis. Lately, CiXi did
not even bother to know the detail. She was relying on someone like Qu to
do the job. However, was it possible that Qu could make decisions against
CiXi intention without her knowledge? Was it possible that Qu was indeed
planning to work with Kang against her wish?

On the other hand, was it bad to restore GuangXu? After all, the reform
she was doing was not so much different from what the Hundred Days
Reform did. She was not against the reform from the beginning. Only that
she was upset that GuangXu dared to call the military force to prevent her
intervention. It was unforgivable. While CiXi was undecided, another event
triggered CiXi's decision.

While Prince Qingqing and Yuan were anxiously waiting CiXi to
remove Qu from the Grand Council, however, after many days, nothing
happened. Prince Qingqing and Yuan became uneasy and concerned. They
decided to launch another blow.

On June 17, CiXi asked Prince Qingqing to come along, and showed an
impeachment memorial to him. CiXi asked him whether he had read this
memorial. Of course, Prince did. Nevertheless, he pretended that he did not.

It was an impeachment memorial from a court official named Yun Yu
Ding. The impeachment said that Qu was allying himself with the Kang's
rebel gang overseas, trying to revive GuangXu's power and presented
additional facts. At that time, CiXi was already convinced that Qu should
not be allowed to stay in the Grand Council anymore. This impeachment
served nothing more than to confirm CiXi's suspicion and therefore and
pushed CiXi toward making a decision. CiXi was trying to find replacement
to Qu, and had identified Zhang Zhi Dong as a candidate. With backup
personnel in mind, CiXi decided it was the time to remove Qu from Grand

Council. Soon, Prince Qingqing drafted an edict for CiXi to take away all titles that Qu had. Qu returned to his hometown. Finally, Yuan's plan to remove Qu worked exactly as he had planned. Now, he wanted to give Cen another blow.

When Cen was taking a sick leave in Shanghai, the news of Qu's dismissal arrived. Cen realized that his alliance with Qu had collapsed completely. Earlier he still had hope that Qu being in the Court could support his return sometimes later. Now even this remote chance was gone.

On August 12, 1907, another memorial arrived in the Court. It was from Duan Fang – one of the officials who went to the Grand Assessment Tour to the West. Duan had long been a rival of Cen. When CiXi exiled to Xian, Cen escorted CiXi all the way from northern China to Xian. CiXi was grateful to Cen, therefore, upon arriving in Xian, offered Cen a position as the Viceroy of Shanxi. At that time, Duan Fang was the Deputy Viceroy of Shanxi, acting as the Viceroy. With Cen's arrival, he had lost his expected promotion. Since then, Duan Fang was resentful of Cen. Since his return from the Grand Tour, he considered himself as an expert of Westernization. He worked closely with Yuan and was eyeing to be Staff of Grand Council. With the removal of Qu, he thought his chance had arrived. He was more than happy to comply with Yuan's request to write the impeachment memorial. By doing so, he could take revenge on Cen, and gain an alliance with Yuan. Without truly finding a cause for the impeachment, he invented one.

The memorial had attached a picture. It was a picture of Cen together with Kang You Wei and Liang Qi Chao, two of the most wanted men in China for the Hundred Days Reform coup. The men in the picture were smiling. Duan had earlier found two separate pictures – one of Cen and the other of Kang and Liang. He asked expert to synthesize these two pictures into one. At that time, few people realized that the pictures could be synthesized. The picture was presented as evidence to CiXi that Cen was a collaborator of Kang.

One event after another bombarded CiXi. She could not think straight anymore. The evidence presented to her was like undisputable facts that left no doubt. Prince Qingqing added, "Cen and Liang were from the same province." In China, people from the same region had a certain affinity. This was what Prince implied.

Since Cen was taking sick leave in Shanghai, and still had not officially on board to his new assignment yet. CiXi issued an edict to remove Cen's assignment. It spelt an end of another chapter of the power struggle in the Qing Court.

Prince Qingqing and Yuan had won a complete victory. Yuan recovered all this titles and positions. Yuan was ready to pick up the reform that he left unaccomplished almost one year ago.

On September 4, 1907, Yuan was appointed as the Staff of Grand Council, a position that he had desired for long time. Finally, he was in the inner circle of Qing Court. He moved his family from Tianjin to Beijing.

On September 16, he celebrated his fifty years of birthday. Media described his birthday party as one of the most elaborated, extravagant for any court official. The avenue leading to Yuan's residence parked full of carriages. Hundreds of the uniformed police officers were nearby to maintain order. Nearly all the court officials in Beijing attended the party, which hosted thousand people. Tents were set up in the plaza in the vicinity to perform opera shows, and other entertainment. Gifts from Emperor and Empress Dowager arrived in special royal carriage accompanied by music band. Western Media reported that Yuan was the most powerful politician in China, although nobody could guarantee how long his power could last under the unpredictable political wind in Beijing.

By the end of 1907, CiXi was approaching seventy three year old. Her health was weakening. Everybody could see that CiXi's days might be ending soon. There was no sign that CiXi wanted to restore GuangXu's power. After CiXi died, who would rule the country became a big question in everybody's mind. Therefore, the fight for the control also intensified.

One day, Prince Qingqing approached CiXi, saying, "I need some help to manage the daily business in the Grand Council. I would like to get an assistant."

The request surprised CiXi. She asked Prince Qingqing whom he had in mind. Prince Qingqing mentioned his son, Zai Zeng. Now CiXi understood Prince's intention. He wanted to bring his son into Grand Council in hope that eventually Zai Zeng would replace him.

CiXi did not refuse him, but said, "Zai Zeng is a good boy, but he is still too inexperienced. Let me think about it."

The second day, when CiXi met Prince Qingqing, she said, "I have thought about the request you made yesterday. I have talked to Zai Feng. He is willing to help you."

Zai Feng was GuangXu's younger brother, although of a different mother. That was the end of conversation. Prince Qingqing then realized that he was in a no-win battle. Prince Qingqing, as CiXi's husband XianFeng's brother, was related to CiXi by marriage. However, GuangXu and Zai Feng were CiXi's sister Rong Er's sons. In addition, Zi Feng's wife was CiXi's niece. They were related to CiXi by blood.

Death of CiXi and GuangXu

In 1908, CiXi's health was deteriorating. The fight for the heir apparent intensified. On November 9, 1908, CiXi and GuangXu held an audience together. It was the last time that they appeared together in the Court audience. The situation did not look very good. CiXi was weak and pale. She could hardly hold herself together. GuangXu was quiet as usual. During the entire audience, she listened but did not say much. Occasionally, she would ask Li Lian Ying to hold her. The officials who were reporting would stop and wait until CiXi could continue. CiXi did not have the concentration to listen what the officials had to say, not to mention to make any decision. The audience lasted only half hour when CiXi claimed that she was tired and dismissed the officials.

After the audience, Prince Qingqing and Yuan met. Both thought the end was near. They tried to understand what would happen if CiXi died. GuangXu was not physically strong, but neither was apparently sick. Was he capable of taking the position without any support from Grand Council, or from the court officials?

Should Prince Qingqing and Yuan pay more attention to GuangXu now, to prepare for the eventuality that GuangXu would be in power?

Yuan immediately discarded this expectation. He knew well that GuangXu would not forgive him. He would be lucky if GuangXu would not kill him.

On the other hand, GuangXu had been away from power for many years. He did not have people loyal to him or he could trust in the Court. He could not count on anyone to execute his orders. Was he able to function as an emperor? Would he call back the remnants of the Hundred Days Reform gangs, such as Kang, who were mostly exile in Japan to come back? Yuan was sure that he could easily amass a group of supporters and replace all the current court officials. The popular voices in China would support him.

156

Yuan was afraid that his days were numbered. Yuan had a plan in his mind.

However, this time, he would not even share it with Prince Qingqing.

On the second day, he went to see Li Lian Ying privately. When Yuan saw him, Li was gloomy at the thought of what he had to face. He seems to be depressed. After all, CiXi was his only supporter in the Court, without CiXi, he was nobody. After casual greeting each other, Yuan asked, "How is our Empress CiXi today?"

Figure 19 GuangXu as a kid

Li squeezed out a forced smile, "I am worried about her. The doctor said that she is very ill, and asked to have a consultation with other doctors."

Li's statement alerted Yuan. The referral of consultation usually meant that the doctor alone could not handle the case, and he wanted to share the responsibility with someone else.

Yuan was silent for a while. He was contemplating whether he should take the next step. After a while, Yuan said, "Li, if Empress CiXi would die, and Emperor GuangXu consolidates his power, what do you think it would happen to us?"

Li Lian Ying was apparently shaken by the prospective. He said, "I cannot speculate. I can only pray that GuangXu would be kind enough."

Li had known GuangXu since he was a child, when he first came to the Forbidden City to be enthroned at four years old. Li Lian Ying played with GuangXu when he was a kid. Nevertheless, since GuangXu was a child, he disliked Li. He called Li ugly. He would play tricks on Li. He would make fun of Li and laughed at his mischief. GuangXu liked to ride on Li's back as a horse. He liked to call Li "Eunuch" even before he knew the meaning of it. It was a child play, but Li did not take it well and felt humiliated.

CiXi used to ask Li to take care of GuangXu. She often asked him how GuangXu was doing. At that time, CiXi's residence was at the west side of the Forbidden City, while Empress XiaoZhen, Emperor XianFeng's formal wife, had a residence at the East side. Sometime, Li would take GuangXu to play in the East Empress' residence. CiXi often inquired Li how XiaoZhen was treating GuangXu, what he ate, what he did. It was the nature care of a mother for kids going to friend's house. Li performed a baby sitter function. However, a habit lasted a life-long. Out of revenge of humiliation, Li would invent or exaggerate GuangXu's childish misconduct and report to CiXi with malice intention to make CiXi angry and to punish GuangXu. GuangXu's dislike of Li grew stronger.

When GuangXu grew older, there was no need for Li to baby sit anymore. However, the old habit of reporting GuangXu's activities continued. Li would inform CiXi about GuangXu's daily activities: What lessons he had on the day, what he learned from his tutor, Weng, and what he did besides studying. Through his miss-interpretation, the gap between CiXi and GuangXu grew bigger. Especially during GuangXu's adolescence, the nature of disobedience as a teenager made the communication between CiXi and GuangXu even more difficult.

When CiXi forced up GuangXu to marry LongYu, whom GuangXu disliked, the relationship between CiXi and GuangXu turned worse. Even though GuangXu reluctantly accepted the marriage, GuangXu kept a distance from her and refused to be with her. Instead, GuangXu chose to stay with Consort Zeng all the time. Li would gossip about Consort Zhen, creating an engulfing gap between Consort Zhen and CiXi, which eventually lead to Consort Zhen's death. GuangXu became even more hateful of Li.

GuangXu despised Li Lian Ying not because he was a eunuch but because the damage that Li inflicted on him by spying on him and distorting or even falsely reporting on him to CiXi was beyond repair. Now finally the payback would come.

Yuan perceived Li's distress, and pushed, "I have a plan that can solve our problems. Do you want to listen?"

Li, his eyes brightened, answered yes. He knew that Yuan was always full of wits.

Yuan produced small paper bag from his pocket, and said, "The only thing you have to do is to mix this into GuangXu's food."

Li was astonished. He froze and tried to understand its implication. Yuan retrieved his bag and said, "Forget what I said."

Li glanced around without seeing anyone nearby and hurriedly he held Yuan's arm, "Give it to me." He took over the bag. That was the night of November 10, 1908.

The next day, November 11, GuangXu, apparently normal in the morning, collapsed after lunch. When the court doctor arrived, GuangXu was already dead. Eunuchs hurriedly notified GuangXu's death to CiXi and LongYu.

LongYu hastily went to Yantai to see GuangXu. After all, she was still GuangXu's spouse; even they did not get along. After the death of Consort Zeng, LongYu's rival for GuangXu's love was gone. LongYu tried to re-approach GuangXu. Even though GuangXu did not accept her, he did not reject her either. Two of them were seeing each other more often. LongYu and GuangXu were cousins. They grew up together and were playmates at childhood. The fact that GuangXu did not love her did not make her enemy.

By the time LongYu arrived in Yantai, GuangXu's quarter, he was already dead. Suddenly she could not control herself and start to cry. Seeing GuangXu lying on his bed, pale, dead, with the expression of suffering, her distaste against GuangXu dissipated completely. In all her life, she was trying to win GuangXu's heart and love, and she failed miserably, although lately, GuangXu was more comprehensive to her. She became hopeful. Now, all the hope was gone. His death was so sudden that she was not prepared to face.

Unexpectedly, she noticed GuangXu was clenching on a piece of paper with something written on it. She forcefully opened GuangXu's tight fingers and retrieved the paper. To her surprise, there were only two words written on it: "Kill Yuan!"

The news of GuangXu's death arrived in CiXi quickly. She was shocked. She suspected that GuangXu was murdered. However, who could have murdered GuangXu? She felt suddenly dizzy. The news made her weak body even weaker.

Despite all the noises to set up an heir apparent, she resisted to do so. In her mind, she wished that GuangXu would continue to reign. Despite everything said about CiXi's animosity against GuangXu, after the initial wrath was over, she did not do anything further to put down GuangXu. There was never an official edict to depose GuangXu. Although the world knew that GuangXu was under house arrest, CiXi continued to issue all the edicts by the name of GuangXu. During the daily morning audience, CiXi insisted that GuangXu would sit by her. She did not want GuangXu to be out of touch. In her mind, if she did not do anything, GuangXu would resume the power automatically when she died. After all, GuangXu was still the Emperor. She hated those rumors portraying her as devil that imprisoned GuangXu. After all, GuangXu was the dear son of her beloved sister – Rong Er.

When CiXi, as Laner, entered the Forbidden City for the first time, she swore that she would bring her family to prosperity. She made Prince Chunqing to marry Rong Er. She gave her brother Guei Xiang a good position in the government. She offered Rong Lu, her cousin, also a position in the military. Later, when Rong Lu proved to be loyal and capable, she promoted him many times. It proved to be the best move that she made in her life. Rong Lu was the one who saved her from the critical situation after her husband XienFeng's death. Rong Lu had been a loyal follower to the end of his life.

After the death of her son, Emperor TongZhi at nineteen, barely old enough to rule the country, she selected her sister's son Zai Tian, later known as GuangXu as the next emperor. She kept her promise to make her family prosperous.

She remembered the day soon after Zai Tian, the future Emperor GuangXu, was born, she visited her sister Rong Er. Rong Er was elated to have a son after her first son died at the age of two a couple of years ago. CiXi was holding Zai Tian and kissed him.

After TongZhi died, CiXi was devastated. She did not have another son. She could not have son anymore. It was not possible for her to remarry. Rong Er's son became her next kin. She discussed with Rong Er to let Zai Tian be the next emperor. At that time, Zai Tian was only four years old. That meant to Rong Er that she would have to give up her dear son and rarely see him again. Even when she did see Zai Tian, she would have to kneel down to him and call him "Your Highness."

However, CiXi would not let her disagree. Soon, Zai Tian moved to the Forbidden City. The day when the procession of escort came to pick up Zai Tian from home, he did not know what was going on and crying not to be taken away. Since then, Zai Tian started his long and lonely childhood life in the Forbidden City.

CiXi insisted on Zai Tian calling her "Father." Out of her sympathy, CiXi allowed Rong Er and Prince Chunqing to stay in the Forbidden City with Zai Tian for a while.

Even to this day, CiXi continued to support Prince Chunqing's family. During the recent reform, she had appointed three of GuangXu's brothers, Zai Feng, Zai Xun, and Zai Tau, as the Ministers of the newly created branches of the government.

CiXi felt that she was exhausted. If GuangXu had not died, she would not have wanted to elect an heir apparent, because GuangXu would rule. Now, the matter became urgent, since she knew that she would not live long. There was no time to be lost.

Immediately, she called the Zai Feng and LongYu to come. She instructed them to impose curfew in the Forbidden City without delay. The news of GuangXu's death had to be strictly confidential. Nobody was allowed to go in and out of the Forbidden City. Qing Court imposed the curfew late at night on November 11, 1908.

Next, CiXi selected Zai Feng's son Pu Yi, four years old, as the next emperor. Zai Feng would be the Regent, and LongYu would be the Empress Dowager.

Yes, CiXi knew that Pu Yi was too young. However, she had no choice. Other candidates like Pu Wei, twenty years old, strongly proposed by Prince Qingqing, were distantly related to CiXi by marriage only.

On the other hand, Pu Yi was the son of GuangXu's brother, Zai Feng, although by different mother. Pu Yi, also Rong Lu's grandson, was the closest kin that CiXi had for the candidate of emperor. CiXi owed her life to Rong Lu. Remembering Rong Lu, as CiXi's most loyal follower, CiXi felt that she was paying back to Rong Lu his loyalty for the last time.

Furthermore, CiXi instructed that the edict had to be issued in the name of GuangXu, as his last will, in order to convince the world that it was GuangXu's choice. Therefore, the news of GuangXu's death would be confidential until the edict was released.

Following CiXi's instructions, Zai Feng and LongYu hurried to prepare the edict, and instructed all who had known about GuangXu's death to swear to keep the news confidential under death penalty. At the same time, CiXi would send Prince Qingqing away in a mission so that Prince Qingqing would not be in the Forbidden City when the edict was issued.

On November 11, less than an hour after Zai Feng and LongYu left, CiXi sent Prince Qingqing to inspect the burial ground for CiXi.

Late at night, curfew was imposed in the Forbidden City. On November 13, the edict to appoint Pu Yi as heir apparent was announced to the nation in the name of GuangXu. The edict, served as GuangXu's testament, also appointed his brother, Zai Feng as the Regent, and his spouse, LongYu, as the Empress Dowager.

One day later, on November 14, 1908, Qing Court announced GuangXu's death to the world. Meanwhile, Pu Yi officially became Emperor XuanTong, the new emperor of China. The Chinese calendar was changed as the year one of XuanTong.

On November 15, CiXi died.

The Last Emperor

The news of death of GuangXu and CiXi, within two days, stunned the entire nation like thunder. Rumors were abounding – why GuangXu died one day before CiXi died. Was he murdered? Who murdered him? How Emperor XuanTong and his father, Regent Zai Feng, would rule the country?

Zai Feng was a relatively unknown figure to the nation. CiXi's forty-eight years of iron-fist rule of China was like eternity. An entire generation of Chinese lived without knowing another ruler. China did not know how to react to the end of CiXi era. The government was in standstill. Monumental changes were to come, but nobody knew how it would happen.

Meanwhile, the revolution intensified. There was no more CiXi to hold the country together. The edicts from XuanTong, from Regent Zai Feng, did not go very far. Their authority did not extend much beyond the Province of Zhili. Regent Zai Feng' s number priority was to consolidate royal family' s power. To do so, he had to remove one obstacle first-Yuan Shi Kai.

Regent Zai Feng had the piece of paper written by Guangxi – "Kill Yuan!" He was pondering what to do. He called a family meeting with LongYu, Zai Xun and Zai Tau.

He had suspected as well that Yuan had murdered GuangXu, but he could not figure how. He had questioned the doctor, but the doctor would not say anything more than that GuangXu had died of natural cause -long years of illness. The doctor was afraid to tell the truth because he did not know whether Zai Feng was testing him. Even without the confirmation, Zai was reasonable sure about it based on GuangXu's note. Zai Feng believed that Yuan was dangerous. He had to handle Yuan with care.

Figure 20 Regent Zai Feng and XuanTong (standing)

When he asked Zai Xun and Zai Tau for their inputs, both replied, "Yuan has the control of Beiyang Army. It is still loyal to their commander. To get rid of Yuan, we have to severe him from his Beiyang Army first. There is an old saying that if you cook a frog in the boiling water, it will feel pain and jump. But if you cook the frog in the cold water and slowly heating up, it will not jump. We should handle Yuan step by step. It would take time to assert our control of the Army and Navy. I think the first step to do is to nationalize all the troops. We have already taken steps to do it anyway. We just want to follow through. Only then, we will be able to rule with power. Before we can do this, if we would kill Yuan, it might provoke Beiyang army into revolt."

The situation in the central and southern China was not stable. The revolutionaries were actively sabotaging. Even Qing Court's new army was not very obedient. The Japanese were tightening their control in Manchuria. Fortunately, there was no major incident with Western Powers. However, there was no guarantee how long the peace would last. Everything they did had to be careful, and be sure not to trigger another crisis.

The meeting lasted for hours. They came up with a strategy. First, they would test Zhang Zhi Dong's loyalty, to make sure that if they would deal with Yuan, Zhang would not oppose.

After they secured Zhang Zhi Dong, they would imply to Yuan that he had murdered GuangXu, and coerce him into giving up all his titles and positions, including his control of the Beiyang Army.

Then, Zai Feng would re-organize the cabinet, to put Zai Xun and Zai Tau in charge of the ministries of Navy, Army and all the military schools.

Once they were reasonable sure that they could control the military force, they would take the next steps to handle Yuan, if still necessary.

So far, Zai Feng kept the note from GuangXu in secret. They were afraid that if the news leaked out, Yuan would initiate a strike first. There was an old Chinese saying, "Do not push dog to the corner. He will fight back." They did not have any hard evidence about the murder, and speculated it based on a piece of paper with only two words from GuangXu. There was no signature, no official seal to certify that GuangXu indeed wrote it. They did not have a case. If they made it an open issue, the public could interpret that they framed Yuan. It could give Yuan excuse to revolt. No, they would not risk doing it.

The next day, Zai Feng called Zhang Zhi Dong in. Zai Feng showed GuangXu's note to Zhang Zhi Dong. Zhang was astonished. When Zai Feng asked him how he should handle the case. Zhang commented, "You have not had the time to consolidate your control in the Beiyang army. I am afraid that if you kill Yuan, Beiyang Army could revolt and how you are going to defend?"

This was what Zai Feng was afraid. He asked, "What would you suggest to do then?"

Zhang Zhi Dong said, "I would suggest that for the time being, you can remove Yuan's duties and work on the Beiyang Army until you are reasonably sure that it belongs to the Qing Court."

This was exactly what Zai Feng wanted to hear. He was hoping that Zhang would not defend Yuan. Since the suggestion came from Zhang, Zai Feng could count on Zhang not to oppose the action. Zai Feng issued an edict to strip all Yuan's posts on January 2, 1909.

On the other hand, Yuan was diffident on GuangXu's murder. Rumors were rampant, and speculating three suspects of the murder – CiXi, Li Lian Ying and Yuan Shi Kai. CiXi was dead. Li and Yuan were conspirators. Yuan was afraid that Li would crack under the pressure, and he would confess that Yuan had given his the poison. Yuan could not count on Beiyang Army if the world knew that he was a murderer. Especially the person he murdered was the still beloved Emperor GuangXu. Yuan remembered how his fellow citizens despised him when he betrayed GuangXu. He would enrage the nation if the fact leaked out.

When he received the edict to be stripped all the positions, he knew that the punishment was coming. He did not know what went wrong and how much they had found out. He did not know that GuangXu had written a note to kill him. He did not know what the motivation that Zai Feng stripped his power was. He speculated that GuangXu's doctor might have determined his true cause of death. He was also afraid that Li Lian Ying had confessed his crime. He wondered something worse would follow. He moved his family in a hurry from Beijing to Tianjin. At least, in Tianjin he could escape to the foreign concession, where he could seek protection. Whether he could count on the foreigners to protect him as a murderer, he could not care so much at this moment.

He was afraid that Zai Feng would not be content with the removal of his duties. Even if Li Lian Ying had not confessed, Zai Fen could easily capture him and torture him into confession, whether Zai Feng knew or not about the murder. Without CiXi's protection, Li Lian Ying was nobody. He knew that Li was not the kind of person who could hold the secret for long. Yuan had no time to lose. While he arranged his family to move, he dressed in plain clothes and departed on a third class train to Tianjin alone. The next event further proved to Yuan that his condition was precarious.

When Yuan was stripped the position as the Viceroy of Zhili, his Deputy Viceroy Yang Shi Xiang acted in his position. Before Yuan departed, he sent a telegram from Beijing train station to request Yang to meet him at train station in Tianjin upon his arrival. However, disappointingly enough, only Yang's son showed up to meet Yuan there. Yang's son apologized and told Yuan that it was "inconvenient" for his father to receive Yuan. Yuan immediately realized what this "inconvenience" meant.

Yang's son also passed a telegram to Yuan. The telegram was from his crony, Zhao Bin Jun, the chief of Beijing Police Department. It said that it was safe for Yuan to return to Beijing because the Staff of Grand Council Zhang Zhi Dong already secured the guarantee of his safety from the Regent.

Yuan was touched by the telegram. He had treated Yang Shi Xiang as protégé and promoted him to his current position, and Yang clearly wanted to distance himself from Yuan. Yuan cursed Yang Shi Xiang. "Only at the time of need, you will see truly whom you can count on." On the other hand, Yuan always treated Zhang as a rival. Yet Zhang risked himself to save Yuan's life. How people worked was beyond Yuan's comprehension.

At second thought, he suspected that it was possible that Zhang might lure him back to Beijing on behave of the Regent Zai Feng. Even at this moment, he did not know whether his crime was exposed or not. However, he discarded this notion because he knew Zhang Zhi Dong as a person, and because if Regent wanted to detain Yuan, he could have easily called him into the Court before issuing the edict to remove his duties, which alerted Yuan.

Without even leaving the Tianjin train station, Yuan took the train again back to Beijing. He went straight to Zhang's home and thanked Zhang for his kindness by kneeling down to Zhang. There was no more expression that Yuan could thank Zhang.

After Zhang accepted Yuan's kneeling, he said sadly, "Yuan Shi Kai, you should be very low key and careful now. Zai Feng holds something against you." Zhang said without elaborating further. However, Yuan knew better. He was even afraid that Zhang would say more.

Zhang told Yuan that Zai Feng agreed to spare Yuan, but under the condition that he had to return to his hometown in Henan. Yuan took his advice and went to his hometown the next day. He wanted to get away as far as possible before Zai Feng changed his mind.

Shortly after Yuan left, Qing Court announced the formation of new cabinet: Minister of Civil Service Administration, which also owned the National Police Department – Shan Qi, Minister of Military Administration – Yu Lang, Minister of Treasury – Zai Ze, Minister of Army – Ying Chang, Minister of Navy – Zai Xun, Minister of Justice – Shao Chang, Minister of Industry, Commerce and Agriculture – Fu Lun. All of them were Manchu and all of them were royal family members.

Six hundred miles away from Beijing, Yuan lived a quite live in a small town where he grew up. Since nothing significant happened, he gradually relaxed. At the same time, he was paying attention to what was going on in China. His ambition started to agitate again. He was like a caged tiger that would not sit quietly for long.

On October 10, 1909, over nine months since Yuan last had seen Zhang, one of Yuan's disciples, Yang Du, came from Beijing and visited Yuan. He delivered a letter from Zhang Zhi Dong to Yuan. It was a poem written by Zhang. It implied that after CiXi's death, Manchu royal families had taken all the key positions in the government and put aside the constitution reform that CiXi had hard-pressed. They moved the political trend backwards.

Yuan said, "Zhang must be very sad."

Yang Du whispered, "Zhang cannot be sad anymore, because he died just before I came. He had a disagreement with the Regent during an audience and had a heart attack."

Yuan's eyes were wet.

The reversal of Qing Court's decision to reform met with fierce resistance all over China. The people were completely disillusioned. The revolutionaries gained momentum. Only Manchu officials continued to put down the revolution uprisings, and persecute revolutionaries. Han officials obeyed on surface but were reluctant to do so.

In February 1910, there was a Guangzhou uprising. Although Qing suppressed it successfully, however, it was significant because the Qing's newly trained army of three thousand men joined the uprising. The only army Qing Court could rely on was the Manchu's own army – the Bannermen Army. However, it was not disciplined, corrupt and ill equipped.

On April 27, 1911, the revolutionaries launched another uprising in Guangzhou. It also failed. Nevertheless, it stimulated wide spread sentiment of revolution.

In May 1911, Qing Court decided to nationalize all the railroads in southern and central China, and sell them to foreigner bankers to raise money. The decision resulted in large-scale protests. Hundred thousands of protesters were marching on the streets to demand Qing Court to reverse the edict. "Protecting the railroad" organizations were set up in all the provinces affected. Qing Court resolved to suppress the protests. It pulled the last trigger of revolution.

The momentum of the protest was so large that the uprising spread beyond the hub of the revolutionaries in coastal provinces. On September 7, 1911, Viceroy of Sichun ordered the arrest of leaders of the "Protecting the railroad" organizations, the scale of protest escalated. The protesters destroyed electrical wire posts and many public utilities.

On September 25, County Rong in Sichun declared independence from Qing Court. Qing Court sent Duan Fang to suppress the disturbance. Meanwhile, in Wuhan, downstream of Yangtze River from Sichun, the revolutionaries were planning a large scale uprising.

On October 10, unexpectedly a bomb under preparation by revolutionaries exploded. It attracted attention from the authorities. Immediately, polices arrived on the site to crack down. The exposure forced the revolutionaries in the new army to launch the attack before the planned date. Unexpectedly, it ignited the fire of revolution.

By 10 o'clock at night, the revolutionary new army took three routes to attack the Viceroy office and headquarter of the eighth garrison. The Viceroy of Hunan and Hupei escaped. Soon, the revolutionaries controlled the city of Wuchang.

In the next two days, the revolutionaries took two neighboring cities – Hankou and Hanyang, and formed a provisional government of Hupei and declared independence.

Duan Fang, one of the delegates of the Grand Assessment Tour, was killed in the battle in an effort to put down the uprising in Sichun and his troop collapsed. It was the last attempt made by the Qing Court.

By this time, the revolution was spreading like wild fire. Thirteen other provinces, including Hunan, Shanxi, Jiangxi, Yunnan, Sichun, Guangdong and others declared independence. Only four provinces, Gansu, Zhili, Shandong, and Henan vowed their allegiance to the Qing Court. Qing Court was in panic.

On November 1, the Regent asked Yuan to help by restoring Yuan to all his previous posts. Yuan's opportunities came. Two days later, Yuan arrived in Beijing to see the Regent. Now, it was Yuan's turn to be in control. He coerced the Regent, "I will help only if you agree to my condition. You have to dissolve the cabinet and assign me in command." Regent had no other choice but to comply.

By November 16, a new cabinet was formed. Yuan eliminated all the royal family members from the cabinet. Yuan handpicked the cabinet members by himself: Minister of Navy was Sa Zeng Bin. Minister of Army was Wang Shi Zhen. Minister of Industry, Commerce and Agriculture was Zhang Jian. Minister of Treasury was Yen Xio. The list went on. It was a major triumph for Yuan. The depressing cloud of the last year had all but disappeared.

On December 12, 1911, the southern provinces elected Dr. Sun Yat Sen, the leader of the revolutionary party, as the provisional President of the Republic of China, the newly formed name of the country. The Capital of the Republic was Nanjing. On January 1, 1912, the Republic abolished Qing's calendar, the third year of XuanTong, and changed the year to be the first year of the Republic. Dr. Sun's immediate task was to form a republic government. He needed to reach agreement with all provinces declaring independence to support him to form the congress and elect a president. At the same time, the northern China was still under Qing Court's control.

Now Yuan was in command of the Qing Court, he kept his promise to the Qing Court and launched the attack on the revolutionaries. Yuan recovered Wuhan from the revolutionaries. However, the subsequent battles became a stalemate.

In order to avoid further bloodshed, Dr. Sun negotiated with Yuan to ask him to support the revolution. Yuan would agree with the condition attached: That he would be the President of the Republic, and he wanted the Capital in Beijing. Dr. Sun reluctantly concurred. On January 25, 1912, Yuan officially sent telegram to Dr. Sun to support the Republic. Yuan used the Qing Court to bargain with the Republic. Once again, he betrayed his sponsor.

Yuan turned to face the Qing Court to force their abdication. Qing Court was at lost. Yuan negotiated a deal with the Qing Court. The deal allowed Qing Court continued to use the Forbidden City as the residence of the royal family, and maintain the royal titles. The Republic would honor the Qing Emperor as an Emperor, a title without any political substance. The Republic would pay a yearly stipend of four million Yuan, the new Republic money, as Qing Court's expense. The Republic would assign a troop to guard the Forbidden City. It was a very generous abdication condition.

On January 29, 1912, Qing Court held its last audience to announce the acceptance of the Abdication Agreement. In doing so, a dynasty founded in 1636 ended. It lasted 275 years – a respectable life span for a dynasty. Four thousand years of the Chinese dynasty political system also ended together with Qing. China entered the mainstream of modern age.

The Last Days of An Empire

Epilog

Comparing to the fate of Tsar of Russia and French King Louis XVI after the revolution, Qing Court was lucky. The Republic not only spared the royal family of the death penalty, but also honored the title of emperor and allowed the royal family to continue to stay in the Forbidden City with a considerable stipend. The Republic funded the construction of GuangXu's mausoleum in the Western Qing Tombs. The Qing royal family stayed in the Forbidden City until 1924, when the warlord Feng Yu Xiang drove them out.

Even the revolutionaries like Dr. Sun Yat Sen praised Emperor GuangXu for his educational reform package that allowed China to learn more about Western culture. Dr. Sun Yat Sen also visited the Regent Zai Feng, acknowledging that he had refused the Japanese lure to cooperate.

People did not hate the Qing rulers as much as the Russian or French hated their rulers. It is true that Empress CiXi was a dictator. However, she was a tyrant nor cruel. Meanwhile, GuangXu was a respected emperor. Some historians consider that he was the first Chinese ruler to implement policies of modernization and capitalism. His achievement was only limited by his imperial power.

After the establishment of the People's Republic of China, Communist historian Fan Wen Lan called Emperor GuangXu "the Manchu Noble, who could accept Western thinking." In Communist China, the royal families were treated with courtesy and some of them were elected as members in the National People's Congress Standing Committee, National Commission of Ethnic Committee. The Communist leaders like Mao Ze Dong and Zhou En Lai would occasionally receive the royal families and ordered their protection during the Culture Revolution.

However, many Manchu nobles, without having a skill to make a living on their own, and not knowing how to manage their fortunes, quickly exhausted what they had, once they lost the financial support from Qing Court. The heir apparent Fu Hui exiled together with his father Prince Duan to Xinjiang, lived his life dirt-poor, became blind and died in 1942 at fifty-seven. When he died, his family did not even have money to bury him.

Emperor XuanTong, or Pu Yi, was captured Russians after the World War II, and imprisoned in Russia for five years. In 1949, he was extradited back to China and served in the re-education camp for war criminals and was released in 1959. The Communist government assigned him to work for several years in a botanic garden, and then transferred him to a research institute for historical records. Later he was elected as a member of the CPPCC (Chinese Political Party Consultative Committee) until he died in 1967 at sixth one.

To resolve the riddle of GuangXu's death, his body was exhumed in 2008. The forensic tests revealed that the level of arsenic in the Emperor's remains was hundred times higher than normal. In order to discard the environmental factors, his wife LongYu's body next to him was also exhumed. Her body was free from arsenic. It removed the possibility of environment contamination. Scientists concluded that such high concentration of poison near stomach could only mean that the poison was administered in a high dose at one time, rather than slow poisoning over the long time as some had suggested. GuangXu was indeed physically weak and not healthy but his physical weakness did not prompt his sudden death. Therefore, it was established that GuangXu was indeed murdered.

Did the doctor who visited GuangXu at the deathbed know? Most likely, he knew. Dared he say anything about it? Surely, he dared not. Anyone would know that only high-powered person could have committed the murder. How would he have the courage to disclose the murder to the potential murderer, knowing that he could be silenced immediately?

Out of three candidates who could have murdered GuangXu, Empress CiXi was the least likely one. Even though she confined GuangXu, she never officially deposed him. During her reign, she continued to ask GuangXu to appear in the daily court audience. When she issued edicts, she continued to do so in GuangXu' s name. After one attempt, she did not try to set up another heir apparent. The reform she implemented later was no different from what GuangXu pushed during his Hundred Days Reform.

Most importantly, she did not have the motivation to murder GuangXu when she was about to die. She could gain from it except a bad reputation.

Furthermore, she was very protective of her blood family. GuangXu was her dear sister – Rong Er's son. The reason that she set up Pu Yi as the heir apparent when she was dying was because Pu Yi was her brother's grandson – a candidate most closely related to her by blood. Moreover, she did it only when she learned that GuangXu had died. That much was clear.

What would happen if GuangXu had not been murdered? It could only leave us to the imagination. Based on some reasonable speculation, GuangXu would not have formed an all-Manchu cabinet. Once he commented sarcastically, "What could the inept Manchus do to strengthen China?" He would have been more open to share his power, and have recalled Kang You Wei and Liang Qi Chao to continue with his aborted reform. A constitution would have been set up according to Kang's plan, which was well publicized. Constitutional Monarchy system could have been implemented shortly.

GuangXu would not have nationalized the railroad to fund his Court. It would then not have triggered the events of revolution. GuangXu had much sympathy from the West, and foreign aggression could have been reduced. However, the Japanese aggression would not stop.

GuangXu might survive the Republican revolution, but he would not survive the Japanese aggression and the following communist revolution. The China today would probably be not much different.

At the downfall of Qing Dynasty, XuanTong was just a kid. He could not be responsible for anything. People also realized that there was no lack of efforts to reform. Just the task was too big beyond the capability of Qing Court.

Yuan played an entirely different role. Yuan was a capable administrator. He had done many good things for the modernization of China. However, he was over driven by his ambition that ruined his reputation. Yuan was not content to be only a president. He wanted to be an emperor. Not long after he became the president, he abolished the congress and established himself as an emperor. The entire country was outraged. He soon died out of depression.

He had betrayed Emperor GuangXu in the Hundred Days Reform. He had betrayed Regent Zai Feng to turn toward the Republic. He had betrayed the Republic by installing himself as the new emperor of China.

After the republic revolution, the aggression from the foreign powers stopped except from Japan. Russia was preoccupied with her own revolution. The European Powers were busy engaging in the World War I. However, the existing terms of the unequal treaties continued until 1947, the founding of People' s Republic of China. For the first time in more than one hundred years, China had regained her complete sovereign rights. This is one of the reasons that Mao Ze Dong, the founding father of the People' s Republic, is so revered in China. He might have made many mistakes, but comparing his contribution to regain China' s sovereignty, his mistakes can be forgiven by his countrymen. Britain returned Hong Kong to China in 1997 when ninety nine years of the lease was expired in the New Territory north of Hong Kong. The last vestige of Western Power aggression was cleared.

However, Japan' s assault on China intensified after the Republic revolution. She created the incident after the incident to provoke China.

In 1914, Japan declared war against Germany and marched troops into Shandong and took control of Germany's concessions. In 1918, Japan expanded her control to northern Manchuria. Soon, Japan set up a puppet government using the deposed Qing last emperor Pu Yi as a puppet. In 1937, Japan launched full-scale warfare against China, which was four years before the World War II.

Japan used the same strategy to attack the Russian battleships in Port Arthur in 1904 to attack Americans in the Pearl Harbor in 1941. However, this time, Japan was not so lucky. The attack enraged the United States into declaring war against Japan, that she had no chance of winning.

Japan committed fatal mistakes by her aggression on China and the United States. Japan was dragged into prolonged warfare with China because of her extension and population. Japan occupied only cities in China, but lacked resources to control expansive rural areas. Her occupation did not extend much more beyond the cities she occupied. Japan could not defend herself in constant guerrilla warfare launched from rural areas.

Japan' s attack on U.S. carried no meaning. U.S. quickly rebuilt her navy, and counter attacked. With inferior resources, Japan could not hope to win in the long term.

An alternative strategy for Japan was to occupy the East Siberia of Russia. Russia was fully engaged with the war in her west front. She could barely defend her East. Japan could easily have taken the East Siberia, which is twice as big as Japan. The area was thinly populated and full of natural resources. Japanese could migrate and settle there in large numbers. Without entering the war against the U.S., Japan would not have suffered defeat, and by the end of World War II, Japan could have continued to hold onto Taiwan and Sakhalin Island. U.S. would have supported Japan to defend against the next enemy -Soviet Union. The world today would be much different.

The hundred and fifty years of humiliation and suffer in China created a deep psychological imprint in Chinese mind. It was manifested in the anti-imperialism reaction in the early phase of Communist rule. Inevitably, the Korea War was viewed as another aggression by the Western Power. This time, it was the United States. Unfortunately, many Westerns mistook it as Communist aggression. However, it is not.

Mao Ze Dong's Great Leap Forward movement from 1958 to 1961, having a slogan "To catch up with Britain in 15 years," also reflected his anxiousness to advance country's industry. The movement was a feat that had the right motivation, but wrong methodology. The movement carried the same psychology as GuangXu's Hundred Days Reform. Only after 1980, it seems that China has finally figured out a way and is moving along uninterrupted for thirty years to make a real progress to improve the fundamental strength of the country.

The communist system in China today is an autocracy system. However, it is not much different from the dynasty system in thousand years of Chinese history. People have the basic rights and freedom except the freedom of election, and the rights to be against the government. All the officials are appointed rather than elected. The State Council, which reports to the President of China, today is not so much different from the Grand Council in the Qing Dynasty. Five members of the Premier of the State Council are equivalent to the staffs of the Grand Council. The President of China is produced by the Party as opposed the emperors were chosen from the royal family. Today, the only way to have a political career is through the party, also similar to the Imperial Literature System that exerted the Confucius philosophy to the potential candidates. People still look upon the government to take care of them, in contrast to the concept in the West that people consider government officials as servants. The communist regime can continue to be in power as long as it can provide the people decent living conditions. Therefore, history indeed provides a meaningful lesson to understand the present and to predict the future.

Who was Who

Alexei Kuropatkin	(1848~1925) Russian Minister of War and General during the Russo-Japanese War
Alfred Gaselee	(1844~1918) General of British Army and Commander of the Eight-Nation Alliance army
Cen Chun Xuan	(1861~1933) Viceroy of Guangdong and Guangxi. A tough administrator nicknamed "The butcher of officers" due to his persistent prosecution of corrupted officers. Yuan's rival.
Claude Maxwell McDonald	(1852~1915) British diplomat and ambassador to China during the Eight-Nation Alliance invasion
Consort Zhen	(1876~1900) Emperor GuangXu's most favorable consort. She was killed when fell into a well.
Count von Waldersee	(1832~1904) Chief of Imperial German General Staff and German commander of the Eight-Nation Alliance army
Dai Hong Ci	(1853~1910) Secretary of Interior, Member of the Grand Assessment Tour

The Last Days of An Empire

Der Ling   (1885~1944) Daughter of a Manchu Lord Yukeng,
                        Empress Dowager's lady-in-wait and translator

Dong Fu   (1839~1908) the Muslim Army commander during Eight-
Xiang   Nation Alliance invasion

Duan Fang   (1861~1911) Viceroy of Hunan, Member of the Grand
                        Assessment Tour. He was killed in suppressing the
                        Railroad protection riot.

Edward   (1840~1929) British admiral and Commander of the
Seymour   Eight-Nation Alliance army

Emperor   (1875~1908) Son of Prince Chunqing and CiXi's sister
GuangXu   Yong Er. He was the ruler of China for thirty three years
                        by name only.

Emperor   (1856~1875) CiXi's son with Emperor XianFeng. He died
TongZhi   of smallpox at the age of 19.

Emperor   (1906~1967) The last emperor of China named Pu Yi. He
XuanTong   was Guei Xian's grandson. Later, Japanese used him and
                        installed him as a peppet emperor for Manchukoku. After
                        Japanese surrender, he was tried as a war criminal, and
                        spent 10 years in jail. After his release, he became a
                        member of the Political Consultative Conference in the
                        Communist China.

Empress CiXi   (1835~1908) Empress Dowager, Laner, Consort Lan,
                        mother of Emperor TongZhi. She ruled Qing Dynasty for
                        48 years.

Empress LongYu	(1868~1913) Yehenara Jingfen; Emperor GuangXu's wife; Empress Dowager of the last Emperor XuanTong.
Empress XiaoZhen	(1837~1881) Emperor XianFeng's wife
Guei Xian	CiXi's brother; Empress Lonny's father
Harry Smith Parkes	(1828~1885) British diplomat
Henry Pottinger	(1789~1856) First Viceroy of British Hong Kong
Huizheng	CiXi's father
Kang Guang Ren	Kang You Wei's brother, killed in the Wuxu coup
Kang You Wei	(1858~1927) The leader of the failed Hundred Days Reform. Later, exiled to Japan.
Li Hong Zhang	(1823~1901) The most important court official in late Qing. Viceroy of Zhili. Commander of the Beiyang Army and Navy. Chief architect of Chinese modern industries. Chief negotiator of most treaties with foreign powers.
Li Lian Ying	(1848~1911) CiXi's head of eunuchs.
Liang Qi Chao	(1873~1929) Kang You Wei's disciple; a leader of the Hundred Days Reformer
Liu Kun Yi	(1830~1902) Viceroy of Liangjiang

Lu Zhuan Lin   (1836~1910) Viceroy of Guangdong; Grand Council

Prince   (1838~1917)Yikuang;   direct   descent   of   Emperor
Qingqing   QianLong; Chief of Staff of Grand Council; During the
                Boxers, he was strongly against the Boxers

Prince   (1840~1891) Emperor XianFeng's brother, GuangXu's
Chunqing   father, married to Yong Er;

Prince Duan   (1856~1922) Emperor XianFeng's niece; married to
                CiXi's brother's daughter; Empress LongYu's sister

Prince   (?~1861) Sushun's brother; Killed by CiXi in the coup.
Zhengqing
(Duanhua)

Qu Hong Ji   (1850~1918) Staff of Grand Council in the last days of
                CiXi; Yuan Shi Kai's rival.

Senggelinqin   (1811~1865) Mongolian general in Qing Court during the
                second opium war. He was killed in the battle to put down
                Nian uprising in Shandong.

Shao Ying,   (1861~1925) Deputy Minister of the Commerce
                Department. One of the members of Grand Assessment
                Tour.

Sheng Xuan   (1844~1916) Industrialist, Nanyang Minister of
Huai   Commerce, Proponent of the Self Protection Movement.

Sushun	(1816~1861) The most powerful Court Official during Emperor XianFeng. He was defeated by CiXi after XianFeng died.
Tie Liang	(1863~1938) Staff of Rong Lu, Staff of Grand Council, one of the Manchu military strategist
Tongjia	CiXi's mother
Weng Dong He	(1830~1904) Emperor GuangXu's private tutor. He had strong influence on GuangXu.
Xu Shi Chang	Staff of Grand Council in the last days of CiXi; Yuan Shi Kai's friend
Yang Shi Qi	Yuan Shi Kai's crony
Ye Ming Chen	(1807~1859) Viceroy of Guangdong before the second opium war. He was captured by British and sent to India. He died in India.
Yong Er	CiXi's younger sister, married to Prince Chunqing. Emperor GuangXu's mother.
Yong Lu	(1836~1903) CiXi's cousin; commander of Qing Army during Eight-Nation Alliance invasion.
Yu Xian	(?~1901) the Viceroy of Shandong who supported the Boxers; later was executed as the responsible for the

The Last Days of An Empire

Boxer Rebellion

Yuan Shi Kai	(1876~1929) Viceroy of Zhili; first President of the Republic of China
Zai Feng	(1883~1951) Regent; father of last Emperor XuanTong; GuangXu's brother
Zai Tau	(1888~1970) GuangXu's brother; Minister of Army; Council of the People's Liberation Army; Representative of National People's Congress
Zai Xun	(1886~1949) GuangXu's brother; Minister of Navy
Zai Ze	(1976~1929) Married CiXi's brother Guei Xian's daughter JingRong; Member of the Grand Assessment Tour.
Zai Zhen	(1876~1947) Prince Qingqing's son. He was the Minister of Industry, Commerce and Agriculture.
Zeng Guo Fan	(1811~1872) Founder of Xiang Army. Li Hong Zhang's mentor. He defeated Taiping Rebellion.
Zhang Zhi Dong	(1837~1909) Viceroy of Hunan. He built many industries in central China.
Zhou Fu	(1837~1921) Viceroy of Jiangsu and Jiangxi. Later, Viceroy of Guangdong and Guangxi.

Chronological Events

1635	Formation of Qing Dynasty
1644	Qing Dynasty replaced Ming as China's ruler
1840~1842	First Opium War
1851~1864	Taiping Rebellion
1853	Zeng Guo Fan organized Xiang Army
1858~1860	Second Opium War
1858	China conceded East Siberia to Russia
1862	Emperor XianFeng died. CiXi was in power
1865~1866	Nian uprising
1866	Japan Meiji Restoration
1871	Tianjin Church Incident
1874	Japan invaded Taiwan
1875	Zhao Shang Shipping Company formed

The Last Days of An Empire

1875	British invaded Yunnan
1880	Japan annexed Okinawa
1882	Korean uprising
1883	France invaded Vietnam
1888	Formation of Beiyang Navy
1888	Emperor GuangXu's marriage
1894	CiXi 60th birthday
1894~1895	Sino Japanese War
1897	Russia invaded Manchuria
1898	Hundred Days Reform
1900~1901	Eight-Nation Alliance invasion
1904~1905	Russo-Japanese War
1904	Formation of Bao Ding Police Department
1908	CiXi and GuangXu died
1911	Broke out of Republican revolution
1912	Emperor XuanTong abdicated
1945	End of Japanese aggression in China
1947	Formation of the People's Republic; Abolishment of all unequal treaties
1997	British returned Hong Kong to China

The Last Days of An Empire

www.ingramcontent.com/pod-product-compliance
Lightning Source LLC
Chambersburg PA
CBHW062146280526
45788CB00001B/333